❖ HARRIET HARGRAVE ❖
HEIRLOOM
MACHINE
QUILTING

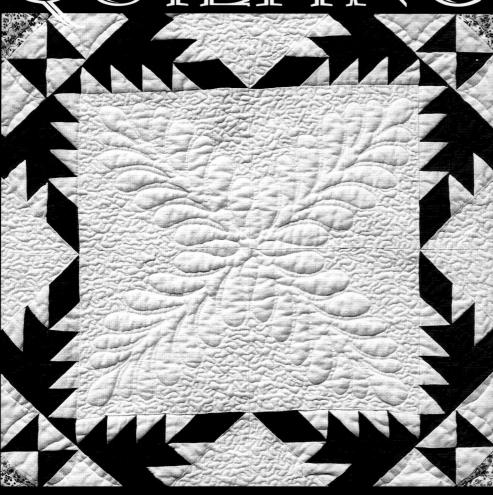

*A Comprehensive Guide to Hand-Quilted
Effects Using Your Sewing Machine*

2

We have made every attempt to properly credit the trademarks and brand names of the items listed in this book. We apologize to any that have been listed incorrectly and would appreciate hearing from you.

Bernina is a registered trademark of Fritz Gegauf, Ltd. Carb-Othello is a registered trademark of Schwan-Stabilo. Charcoal White is a registered trademark of the General Pencil Co. Cotton Choice is a registered trademark of Sterns Technical Textiles Co. Clearly Bleached and Clearly Unbleached are registered trademarks of Morning Glory Products. Cotton Classic is a registered trademark of Fairfield Processing Corporation. Dawn is a registered trademark of Proctor and Gamble. DBK is a trademark of Inglis Publications Products. DMC is a registered trademark of the DMC Corporation. Easy Wash is a registered trademark of Airwick Industries, Inc. Ensure is a registered trademark of Sterns Technical Textiles Co. Exacto is a registered trademark of Hunt Manufacturing. Extra Loft, Low Loft and Hi Loft are registered trademarks of Fairfield Processing Corporation. Fade-Away is a trademark of White Sewing Products Co., a division of White Sewing Machine Co. Glazene process is a registered trademark of Sterns Technical Textile Co. Heirloom is a registered trademark of Hobbs Bonded Fibers. Ivory Clear Dishwashing Soap is a registered trademark of Proctor and Gamble. Jubilee is a trademark of Johnson Wax, Inc. Joy is a registered trademark of Proctor and Gamble. Kanagawa is a brand name of YLI Corporation. Karismacolor is a registered trademark of Berol USA. Kwik Klip is a trademark of Star Tech. Loftguard is a registered trademark of Hoechst/Celanese. Madeira is a registered trademark of Madeira Threads (U.K.) Ltd. Mark-B-Gone is a trademark of Dritz Corporation. Mountain Mist is a registered trademark of Sterns Technical Textile Co. Multi-Pastel Chalks is a registered trademark of the General Pencil Co. Mylar is a registered trademark of E.I. duPont de Nemours & Co. Natesh is a registered trademark of Kaleidoscope. Orvus Paste is a registered trademark of Proctor & Gamble. Old Fashioned is a registered trademark of Sterns Technical Textiles Co. OUIJA is a registered trademark of Parker Brothers Division of Kenner Parker Toys Inc. Palmolive is a registered trademark of Colgate. Pellon is a registered trademark of Freudenberg Nonwovens, Pellon Poly-Down is a registered trademark of Hobbs Bonded Fibers. Quilt-Light is a registered trademark of Sterns Technical Textile Co. Schmetz is a brand name of Ferd. Schmetz GmbH., Germany. Sharpie is a registered trademark of Sanford Corporation. Singer Featherweight is a registered trademark of Singer Corporation. Snowy Bleach is a registered trademark of Airwick Industries, Inc. Stitch Thru is a trademark of EZ International. Sulky is a registered trademark of Sulky of America. Sullivan Metafil is a brand name of Sullivan, Germany. Supracolor is a registered trademark of Caran D'Ache. Swiss Metrosene is a registered trademark of Mettler, Inc. Taos Mountain Traditional and Designer Light are registered trademarks of Taos Mountain Wool Works. Tear-Away is a brand name of Sew Art International. Thermore is a registered trademark of Hobbs Bonded Fibers. Traditional is a trademark of Fairfield Processing. Washout Cloth Markers is a brand name of Dixon/Ticonderoga. Warm and Natural is a trademark of Warm Products, Inc. Wonder Thread is a registered trademark of YLI. Velcro is a registered trademark of Velcro USA Inc.

Published by C&T Publishing
P.O. Box 1456
Lafayette, CA 94549

Photography: *Brian Birlauf*

Developmental editor: *Barbara Konzak-Kuhn*

Technical editors: *Michelle Jurich and Sally Lanzarotti*

Illustrations: *Randy Miyake/Miyake Illustrations and Donna Yuen*

Composition and Electronic Page Make-up:
Irene Morris, Morris Design, Monterey, CA

Library of Congress Cataloging-in-Publication Data
Hargrave, Harriet.
   Heirloom machine quilting : a comprehensive guide
   to hand-quilted effects using your sewing machine /
   Harriet Hargrave. --3rd ed.
      p   cm.
   Includes bibliographical references and index.
   ISBN 0-914881-92-2
   1. Machine quilting.   I. Title.
TT835.H338   1995
746.46--dc20   94-47305
                                              CIP

Printed in Hong Kong

10 9 8 7 6 5 4 3 2

CONTENTS

3

DEDICATION

*This book is dedicated to
my mother, Frances Frazier.
Without her constant support, love,
and dedication to her family,
I would not have the love for quilts
that I share with her, nor the
luxury of pursuing a career in the
areas I love:
teaching, traveling, and quilting.*

INTRODUCTION

The response I received from the first writing of *Heirloom Machine Quilting* exceeded my wildest dreams. Previously, I had spent a great deal of time trying to be low profile and not make waves in the hand-quilting world. In 1986, machine quilting was appearing here and there, but very seldom did quality machine-quilted quilts appear at local and regional shows, let alone at national shows. When I started traveling and teaching nationally in 1985, I introduced the art of machine quilting to anyone who was curious as to how I got my quilts to look hand quilted. In fact they were quilted in a matter of hours using my best friend—my Bernina® sewing machine. I still remember feeling I had to defend and sell the concept in most areas.

Four years later, the national exposure to machine quilting had increased to the point that Caryl Bryer Fallert won the Best of Show at the 1989 American Quilter's Society (AQS) quilt show in Paducah, Kentucky, with her quilt, Corona II: The Solar Eclipse. This coveted award, when given to a machine-quilted quilt, caused quite a reaction—both positive and negative—in the quilt world. Instead of seeing what a magnificent piece it was regardless of technique, many quilters had trouble accepting the fact that it was machine quilted. I look forward to the day when all quilters, hand and machine, look at what the actual quilting lends to the quilt. The quality of the work and the skill that it takes to achieve the final product should be appreciated. I feel that we spend too much energy debating whether machine or hand is best. There are enough quilts in all our heads that need to come out, that as long as the workmanship is of high quality, it should not matter what technique was used.

The first edition of *Heirloom Machine Quilting* contained the general directions to achieve quality machine quilting. I was honored when Caryl Fallert mentioned it in her interview with AQS after winning. She said, "I believe a real breakthrough for quilters came when Harriet Hargrave's book was published with complete and concise directions for machine quilting." Her statement affirmed that I had done what I was hoping to do in that book.

However, after four years on the road teaching, and after hundreds of students have asked thousands of questions, I found that more complete information and guidance was needed. And realizing that I can't be everywhere, and that teachers needed more support, I was delighted to have the opportunity to rewrite the book in 1990.

It is now another four years later, 1994, and I find that there are so many new products that we must update again. I have also fine-tuned my teaching of machine quilting so the success rate is much higher and faster. I wanted the opportunity to share these ideas with the new machine quilters purchasing this updated book.

I find it amazing how nine years ago machine quilting was such a disliked concept, and today, the classes keep filling more than ever. Quilters just don't have the time to finish every quilt they make by hand. The concept that real quilts are quilted by hand is very unfair to today's quilters. No longer do we have long evenings to quilt and mend around the fire as our grandmothers did. We are constantly on the go with careers, children's activities, etc. The car, television, and technology of today has ended the era of spare time. It is no wonder that the popularity of machine quilting keeps growing by leaps and bounds. When you can complete a quilt in hours by machine instead of months by hand, and it looks every bit as beautiful, is it any wonder that machine quilting is where it is today?

Suellen Meyer wrote a research paper for AQSG about early machine quilting. Just for your information, I thought I would include some of her little known facts about the tradition of machine quilting:

❖ *When the sewing machine was introduced it cost $125.00; at a time when the average annual family income was $500.00. This is equal to purchasing a car today. The machine was a true status symbol.*

❖ *By 1859, machine quilting was being entered in California fairs. By 1860, it is reported that about half of the quilts dated after 1860 are machine pieced, and that the edges of both appliqué and pieced quilts were commonly finished by machine.*

❖ *During the period of 1865-1900, 10% of all quilts made bear some machine appliqué or quilting on the surface.*

❖ *By the end of the century, machine quilting was not looked upon favorably in fashionable circles.*

When someone tells me that traditional quilts are only hand made, I ask for a definition of traditional.

I wish you the best of luck in your pursuit of mastering machine quilting. It will provide you with limitless hours of enjoyment and satisfaction and will let you get many more quilts out of your head and onto your beds and walls, where they can be enjoyed by all.

❖ PART ONE ❖
GETTING
READY

WORK SPACE AND EQUIPMENT

Y ou are not machine quilting, you are hand quilting with an electric needle. If you think about it this way, you will understand why your work space is so important. The space and equipment you use for machine quilting is as important to your success as that for hand quilting. Maybe more so, since machine quilting creates much more bulk and many maneuvering problems. Your work space should be in a well-lit room that can accommodate a large quilt.

The way you set up your machine makes a real difference in ease of quilting. One of the most important considerations for your workroom is owning a cabinet or extension table for your machine. If your machine is set up in a portable situation, you do not have enough support for the bulk of the quilt. The quilt tends to fall off the side and back of the machine while quilting, or gets caught at the front edge. This necessitates using your hands to support the bulk so stress is not put on the needle while quilting. If your hands are occupied with the quilt, they cannot be at the needle creating the quilting stitches. That bulk must be supported by a table surface in order to free your hands. Another problem is the lack of space for your hands to guide the fabric where it is needed during quilting. Your fingers may fall off the edges of the machine, which hinders your ability to make even, consistent stitches. You will feel yourself tightening up as you work a pattern, waiting in anticipation of falling off and losing control. If the machine is lowered into a cabinet, the table surface is level with the throat plate of the machine. The table supports the quilt, leaving your hands free to quilt. Your hands

will not slip off the edge of the machine as you move the quilt around under the needle. If you go shopping for a cabinet, sit directly in front of the needle. Many models of cabinets center you with the machine, making you reach slightly to the left to control the fabric going through the needle. This causes undue stress on your back and shoulders, distorts your vision, and generally makes the quilting process more difficult. Cabinets such as these should be avoided. Extend your working surface by placing additional tables around the cabinet if necessary. Place one behind the machine and one to the left of the cabinet, so the quilt cannot fall onto the floor and drag against the needle while quilting.

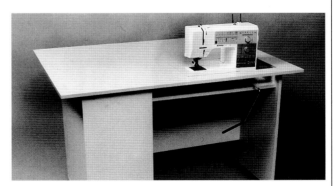

FIG. 1.1 Level sewing surface

If owning a cabinet is not feasible, you can purchase an extension table, such as the one in Figure 1.2. If you are relegated to sewing on the dining room table or you just don't have room for a cabinet, this inexpensive, portable system may be your solution (refer to the source list on page 176). This 48" x 24" extension uses a Parsons insert and fits any brand of machine. The legs adjust to accommodate the height of your machine.

You can create your own extension by going to the lumber yard and purchasing a sheet of masonite or Formica™ covered counter-top material. Look for a product that has a slick surface, which allows the fabric to glide easily. Try to avoid wood, as fabric tends to drag and wood varnishes tend to be slightly sticky. You will need a piece that extends out from the front of the machine about 4", to the left 24"-36", and behind the machine 18"-24". Make a template of the arm of your machine and transfer it onto the material you have chosen. Cut an opening so that it will fit tightly around the arm of your machine. Cut dowels or blocks of wood to the proper height and screw onto the surface for legs. This gives you an excellent working surface that will support your quilt and enable you to move your hands freely as you quilt.

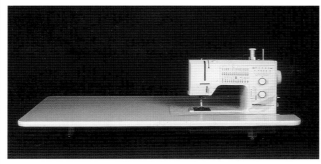

FIG. 1.2 Extension table

Equally important is your chair. If you do not sit properly, machine quilting strains your back and upper arms. Purchase a high-quality secretarial chair. It should have five legs, instead of four, to prevent tipping. Check that the size of the seat fits your body. If the seat is too small, it cuts off circulation to your legs. A pneumatic lift allows you to position the chair height to a comfortable level, with just the lift of a lever. Be sure to check that the chair lifts to a height that allows you to lean over your work slightly, relax your elbows on the table edge, and take the stress off your shoulders and back. (If you are shorter in height, you may need to lower your table or have a small platform on the floor for your foot control, so that you can reach it easily with your foot). The back of the chair should move up and down, as well as forward.

The chair in the photograph has a back that pivots from the seat instead of sliding in and out. This retains the seat depth when you adjust the back. This adjustment is important if you tend to sit in the edge or in the middle of the seat, because it can help eliminate back strain.

This may all seem like a lot of bother, but reaching up with your arms to place and move the quilt under the needle puts a lot of stress on your back and between your shoulder blades. Also, you have much better vision and control when you look down on your work. Lift your chair high enough so that you can see down on the presser foot and fabric. You need to see the needle going in and out of the hole in the presser foot. Check that the glare from the machine's light bulb does not also cause vision problems.

FIG. 1.3 Secretarial chair

Finally, place your chair far enough back so that you can lean forward. Set your elbows or forearms on the edge of the table, and rest your upper body weight on them. Relax your arms and hands. Place your hands on the quilt as though you are playing a piano. Lift the wrists, keeping the fingertips on the surface, so the fingers are ready to walk wherever you need them. By positioning your hands in this manner, the stress to your wrists is minimal.

If your hands or wrists begin to ache, readjust the height you are sitting and the position of your hands. Your hands should fall forward naturally from the wrists in a relaxed state. If you do experience any discomfort, you may want to wear the therapeutic gloves made to support your wrists.

YOUR SEWING MACHINE

The quality of your equipment makes a big difference in its performance. A machine that has constant tension problems, gets hot after sewing for long periods of time, doesn't have the necessary attachments, or won't sew well using different threads on top and bottom, is not going to give you a rewarding experience. Just as woodworkers do not work with discount tools, machine quilters should not expect to do beautiful work with a lesser-quality machine. Suggested machine features:

❖ Perfect tension adjustment, no matter what combination of threads are put into the machine.

❖ Automatic needle stop, so the needle stops instantly when you stop sewing and does not coast on for two more stitches.

❖ Up and down needle position on command. (My machine allows me to do this with the foot control. One tap puts the needle down into the fabric, another tap brings it up to the highest position. I don't need to remove my hands from the fabric, which helps me control the quilt.)

❖ The ability to sew for hours at high speed without overheating.

❖ High-quality accessories that are made strictly for your machine.

❖ A reputable dealer who will help with minor adjustments, and understand what you are doing.

I do not advise using Singer Featherweights® for machine quilting. The feed dog system is straight, and walking feet do not fit properly on this machine. Walking feet needed for machine quilting are designed for a zigzag system, and are too wide for the narrow dogs on the Featherweight. The feed dogs do not drop, making work with a darning foot more difficult. There is very little space available inside the arm of the machine for any bulk to fit. Finally, the motor is small. You can cause excess wear and tear on a machine that is not built to run at high speeds for long periods of time. Keep your Featherweights for piecing and general sewing.

Before starting the exercises in the upcoming chapters, prepare your machine. First, clean it thoroughly inside and out. Most sewing machines seldom get cleaned and polished externally. Remember that your machine lives in your house just like any other appliance, and collects grease and dirt on its surface. Thoroughly clean the surfaces, and wax them. If your machine has a steel base, use a silicone car wax and buff to a high gloss. But do not get wax products on the throat plate, as it may cause discoloration. If your machine's housing is plastic, use Jubilee™ kitchen wax or hot-tub wax. This waxing process allows the fabric to glide smoothly and quickly through the machine. Refer to your manual, or ask your dealer where you should clean and oil. Clean the lint from your machine after each bobbin is emptied, or the lint pulls the oil from the metal and causes excess wearing. Keep the machine well-oiled, but not over-oiled. I suggest every time you change the bobbin, you should clean the bobbin case and feed dog area, and oil very lightly the race, shuttle, and hook areas. If your machine suddenly sounds different, then stop, clean, and oil it. It generally lets you know when it is "hungry" for lubrication. Don't forget to clean the bobbin case. Lint builds up inside the case where the bobbin spins. Every once in a while, slide a coarse piece of thread under the tension clip and pull out any lint or tiny fibers that may have lodged under it. These fibers distort the bobbin tension (Figure 1.4).

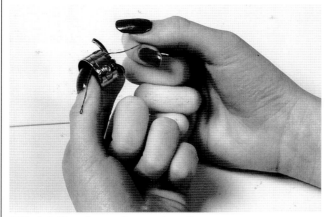

FIG. 1.4 *Cleaning under tension clip*

Machine quilting can be hard on a machine, so extra care is warranted. Even the "non-oiling" machines need extra oil when put through this process. Take them to the dealer at the first sign of any trouble, such as a foreign noise. Have your dealer show you the best way to care for your equipment when it is used for this purpose.

Tension is a mystery to many sewers. I feel that dealers have done us a disservice by not teaching us to adjust tension properly. You should know what the dials are, and how to use them. The numbers are there for reference when adjusting. Experiment with your machine for a few minutes to get comfortable with their function.

One process that can really affect tension is the way your bobbin is wound. When winding the bobbin, be sure it is winding smoothly and evenly, and that the thread is being wound tightly. Loose, unevenly wound bobbins cause poor stitch quality.

Identify the tension adjustment dial on your machine. When doing any type of machine work, make yourself comfortable with tension adjustments to make the machine work properly with different types and combinations of threads. There is no magic in thread tension, and many service calls can be eliminated if you have a thorough understanding of how tension works.

Sew a row of stitches in two layers of fabric. Correct tension is evident when both threads are linked together in the center of the layered fabrics (Figure 1.5a). Figure 1.5b shows the bottom thread being pulled tight. This indicates the top thread is too loose, or the bobbin thread is too tight. Figure 1.5c shows the top thread being pulled tight. This indicates the top thread is too tight, or the bobbin thread is too loose.

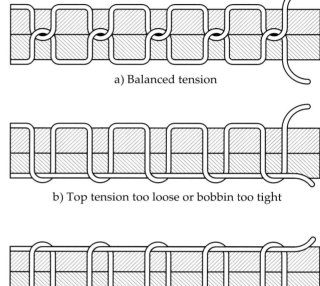

a) Balanced tension

b) Top tension too loose or bobbin too tight

c) Top tension too tight or bobbin too loose

FIG. 1.5 *Effects of bobbin tension*

When excess thread is looped in the bobbin area, it may not indicate a bobbin thread problem. The top thread might be too loose, allowing the race mechanism to gather the loose thread beneath the fabric and prevent stitches from forming properly.

When quilting using cotton thread in the top and bobbin, tension adjustments are minimal, if needed at all. When using nylon in combination with cotton, various tension adjustments may be necessary.

Always adjust the top tension first. Many stitch problems can be corrected simply by loosening the top tension. The smaller the number, the looser the tension; the higher the number, the tighter the tension. Adjust by one-half numbers at a time. Never make severe adjustments. If the top tension is too loose, large loops of top thread form on the bottom of the fabric. If the problem isn't resolved with top tension adjustments only, then adjust the bobbin tension, keeping a balance to accommodate the project and materials you are working on. Tensions can change depending on the type and thickness of the batting you are using. Check the stitch quality on a sample of each batting, before quilting, to make the necessary adjustments.

You can check your own bobbin tension and correct it if necessary. With the high speed and long duration of sewing times, bobbin tension can work itself out of adjustment. Knowing how to check and adjust it can save a lot of time and grief.

Thread a full bobbin into the bobbin case. Make sure it is threaded properly (check your manual to see if the bobbin spins clockwise or counter-clockwise). Most bobbins spin clockwise as you are looking at it. This allows the thread to come off the bobbin then go back on itself as it enters the slit and goes under the tension clip (Figure 1.6).

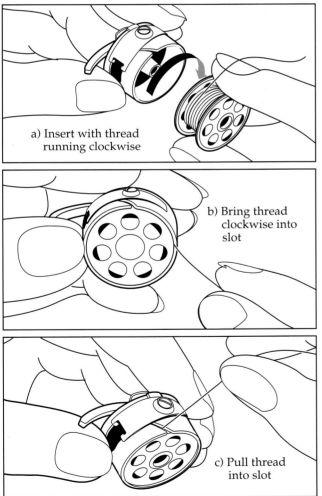

a) Insert with thread running clockwise

b) Bring thread clockwise into slot

c) Pull thread into slot

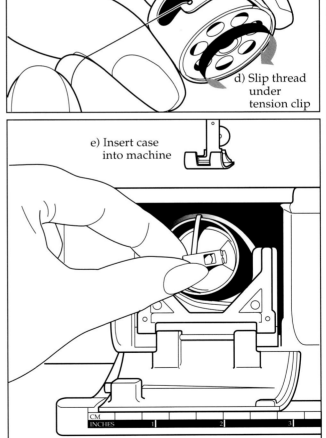

d) Slip thread under tension clip

e) Insert case into machine

FIG. 1.6 *Correct threading of bobbin*

Let the bobbin case hang freely by the thread. It must not slide down by its own weight, but when you jerk your hand lightly upward, yo-yo style, it should gently fall. If it doesn't move at all, the tension may be too tight. If it falls easily, it is probably too loose. This is only a general starting point for the bobbin tension. Now you will need to fine tune the tension for your particular machine. No two machines use exactly the same tension settings.

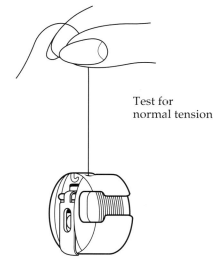

Test for normal tension

FIG. 1.7 Test for normal tension

The large screw on the tension clip adjusts the tension. Turn it to the right to tighten and to the left to loosen. Remember the old saying, "righty tighty, lefty loosy." Adjust in very small increments until the tension is correct. I look at the screw as if it were a clock face, and adjust the screw in one hour increments. Always make a note of where the tension is set before you begin to adjust the screw. That way you can position the screw back to the original setting when you return to normal sewing. Continue to stitch samples to check that the bobbin is not too tight or the top too loose, or vice versa. Compare your samples to Figure 1.5. You want your stitches to lock in the middle of the layers, not on the top or bottom of the quilt.

Make it a habit to check machine top and bobbin tensions before beginning each project. Keep a journal of what settings your machine requires for each batting you use. You might feel more comfortable purchasing another bobbin case to make these adjustments on, leaving the original bobbin case set for normal sewing.

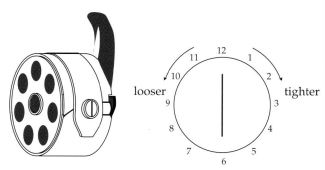

FIG. 1.8 Adjusting tension screw; right to tighten, left to loosen

Also keep in mind that different types and weights of thread require different tension adjustments. A bobbin case set for polyester will be too loose for cotton thread. Polyester has a high thread drag and requires fairly loose tension, whereas cotton thread has no thread drag and sews better if a tighter tension is applied. Thinner weights of thread will slip through the tension clip too freely, and a heavy thread will drag and pull through the same tension setting.

Unbalanced tensions can be used for decorative effects when using different threads. For example, use clear thread on top and black cotton thread in the bobbin. If the top tension is tightened and a large needle is used, the black thread is pulled to the top in tiny loops, creating the look of a tiny, hand-running stitch.

Don't be afraid to experiment and play with your machine. It is a wonderful tool that has the potential to create anything you can imagine. Take classes and sit in on demonstrations from various dealers. They all have tricks you can apply to your machine.

ACCESSORIES

Several accessories available for sewing machines are especially helpful for machine quilting. If you do not find these accessories in your attachment box, check their availability with your local sewing machine dealer.

WALKING FOOT

The walking or even-feed foot is an attachment that allows all three layers of a quilt to move evenly under the foot without shifting or pushing. This foot is a must if you use the feed dogs for machine quilting such as straight-line grid and ditch quilting.

The walking foot is used for any straight-line quilting. This foot fits onto the machine much like a ruffler attachment. There are two "feet" on the attachment. One foot is down when the needle is down and a stitch is being made. The other foot is down when the needle is up and the feed dogs are taking a step. This is controlled by a lever that is connected to the needle clamp screw on your machine. As the lever goes up and down, so does the mechanism of the foot.

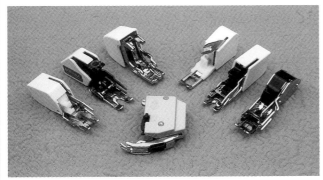

FIG. 2.1 Variety of walking feet

A walking foot reproduces the motion of the feed dogs on top of the fabric. It keeps the top and bottom layers even. The biggest problem in machine quilting is the pushing of the top layer by the presser foot while the feed dogs are gathering up the lining. While the machine is forming a stitch, the feed dog is down and the foot holds the fabric against the throat plate. As the needle comes up, so do the feed dogs. The walking foot then lifts the main foot and sets down another set of feet that line up with the feed dogs. The top fabric feeds evenly with the bottom fabric; the main foot lifts and walks over any fullness without sewing in a tuck or pushing the fabric out of place.

Many sewing machine companies have walking feet available for their machines. For optimal performance, buy the brand that is made for your machine. If your brand does not manufacture a foot for your machine, you will need to get a "generic" foot that fits standard low and high shank machines. There are several different generic feet, and you might have to try different ones before you find one that works adequately with your machine. When installing a walking foot, mount it on your machine and lower the presser bar. Make sure that the inside feeders align exactly with the feed dogs. Otherwise, the pressure does not distribute evenly, and the foot cannot work properly. A poorly fitting walking foot can be worse than no foot at all.

You may encounter a common problem when quilting with a walking foot. Because of the way we piece a quilt block, there are multiple layers of seam allowances that the foot has to pass over. The foot often gets "high centered" on the "lump" these seam allowances create.

The foot cannot release the fabric, so it stalls. You can either lift the presser foot to release the fabric, making sure that the needle is in the quilt to keep position, or you can make an alteration to the foot itself, keeping this from happening at all.

On the foot bottom, there are generally three rubber or plastic feeders that align with the feed dogs: two long ones on the sides of the foot, and one short one behind the needle opening. It is this short feeder that gets caught, as it has to pass directly over the seam. By removing the short center feeder, the height of the seam can pass under the foot. This does not affect the performance of the foot for normal sewing, but it definitely helps in the quilting process (Figure 2.2a).

Another modification that really helps is to open the toes in front of the needle. Using a high-speed cutting or sanding blade, cut through the metal to make a wider opening—making an open-toe walking foot. This allows you to see the ditch more readily and accurately, and is a tremendous help when ditch quilting (Figure 2.2b).

Walking feet that accommodate guide bars are now becoming available. Be sure you have a guide bar that fits both sides of the foot, as you will need to guide off either side of a seam.

FIG. 2.2a
Modified walking foot—
removing feeder on bottom

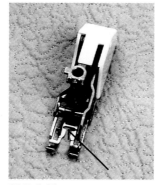

FIG. 2.2b
Modified walking foot—
open toe

Too much or not enough pressure can cause uneven stitches. If your machine has adjustable presser-foot pressure, you may find making slight adjustments to the pressure put on the fabric helps the feeding process.

DARNING FOOT

When using a regular presser foot, it is next to impossible to turn a quilt under the machine to do intricate, fancy quilting designs. This requires free fabric movement under the foot. A darning foot creates the magic of free-motion quilting, and is necessary when attempting to stitch three layers together.

To form a proper stitch, the fabric must be flat against the throat plate as the needle passes through the throat plate hole. The clearances for a properly formed stitch are critical. If the fabric is allowed to lift as the needle comes up, a stitch is skipped. The darning foot rises with the needle, allowing free motion of the work, then lowers with the needle to hold the fabric down on either side of the needle as it enters the fabric. Drop or cover the feed dogs when using this foot.

If your machine brand does not make a darning foot, you will need to fit a generic foot to your machine. When doing this, check to see that the foot works properly. Most of the feet have a spring or bar to the side that rests against the needle clamp screw and gives the foot its jumping action. When the needle is in its highest position, the needle clamp screw should lift this bar, which in turn lifts the foot. If the screw does not go high enough to lift the bar, the foot will not lift, and there will not be enough space between the bottom of the foot and the throat plate foot to allow the fabric to move. When this happens, you know the foot does not fit your machine. There are several different types of feet, and if you persevere, you will eventually find one that works for you.

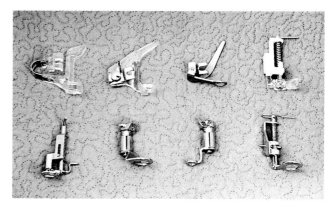

FIG. 2.3 *Variety of darning feet*

Note: Contrary to what you might think, the smaller the darning foot, the easier it is to train your eyes for free-motion quilting. Larger openings in the foot tend to make your eyes stay in the opening, hindering you from looking ahead and preparing for what you will be quilting next. We will discuss this technique in Chapter 12. What you are looking for is a foot that is small enough so the needle cannot skip stitches by bringing the fabric back up when making a stitch. Its size should not hinder your vision when looking at where you are, where you are going, and where you have been. A small foot allows you to see all around it. You do not want to look in the hole while quilting, but on all sides of it.

An open-toe darning foot can also cause problems. The little toes tend to get caught in the thread loops caused by dragging the thread from stopping to starting places. It also tends to push little bits of fabric ahead of the toes, causing tucks against other quilted lines. A closed foot glides smoothly over the surface, working out any fullness.

If possible, try to get a small, round darning foot. If the foot measures $1/4$" from the needle to each edge of the foot, it will be very useful for measuring when echo quilting and working the continuous-curve processes.

If you cannot locate a darning foot for your machine, try using a clear plastic foot, such as an open-toe appliqué foot, and remove all the pressure off the foot by releasing the spring on the top of your machine. Check your manual. A darning spring is also available as a last resort. It is not as effective at compressing the batting while stitching, but it adds finger protection and improves the stitch quality.

Some manuals say to darn without a foot at all. Beware of this. You will notice that when they illustrate this, the fabric is in a hoop. When quilting with a bare needle, you lose maneuverability from the lack of support that the darning foot provides, and your fingers are susceptible to being hit with the needle.

THROAT PLATES

The use of a straight stitch throat (needle) plate helps eliminate puckers and tension problems. The straight stitch throat plate has a tiny round hole to accommodate the needle when straight stitching. (A zigzag throat plate has an oval hole to accommodate the needle swing when zigzag stitching.) Because there is room for only the needle to pass through, a neater and faster stitch is made, enabling the thread to lock tightly.

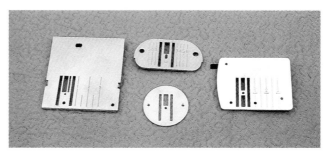

FIG. 2.4 *Straight stitch throat plates*

When sewing straight lines or quilting with a zigzag plate, the needle pushes the fabric down into the oval opening. This hinders the needle's ability to make a clean, locked stitch, and the tension can be thrown off. The bobbin thread tends to lie on the underside and have the appearance of being "couched" by loops of the top thread, especially when using free-motion quilting techniques with a darning foot. Sometimes the stitch will wobble and not look tight.

The straight stitch throat plate gives you a higher quality stitching line when piecing your quilts. When piecing template shapes, it is also very helpful in preventing the first $1/4$" of a point from being "eaten" when the needle pierces the point. When sewing strips together, it eliminates the flanging at the end of strips that is so common. Thus, the seams stay straight and accurate to the very end.

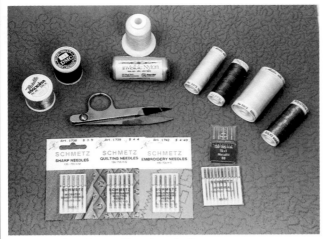

FIG. 2.5 *Threads, needles, thread clips*

NEEDLES

Use only high quality machine needles and start each project with a new needle. Use the needle type, size, and brand recommended for your machine to prevent poor quality and/or skipped stitches.

Size 80/12 needles are the preferred size needle for machine quilting. Do not use needles larger than 80/12s. If you find that needle holes appear in certain fabrics, you may want to change to a 75/11. A finer needle is more fragile, so care must be taken when using it. If you are a beginner, I do not advise using 70s yet.

Schmetz needle company has produced specialty needles for different sewing techniques and threads. One of these needles is called the quilting needle. This needle is tapered and slender, and is made with a true sharp point especially for quilting. This new design allows the needle to pass through the fabric quickly and smoothly, eliminating skipped and uneven stitches. It is excellent for piecing as well as machine quilting. If you are unhappy with the look of your quilting stitches from a standard needle, try this specialty needle and see if it clears up the problems.

When quilting for a long period of time using polyester threads and battings, you might find the thread breaking or even melting.

This can be caused by the high heat buildup from the friction of high-speed sewing through synthetic fibers. If this happens to you, try using a 75/11 blue steel Schmetz stretch needle. It retains a cooler surface when sewing through synthetics. A needle lubricant applied to the needle might also solve your problems.

If you are quilting with rayon thread, the Schmetz embroidery needle gives excellent results. This needle has a deep thread groove down the front of the needle, and a large eye, similar to the topstitching needle. These features protect the rayon thread from excess friction during the stitching process, eliminating breakage and weakening of the thread.

When quilting with metallic threads, use of the Sullivan™ Metafil needle, or the Schmetz Microtex Sharps is a must. These needles are made to eliminate the breakage so common to the brittle and fragile metallic threads.

Many quilters use double needles to create evenly spaced rows of quilting lines. Just remember that a double needle uses two top threads, but only one bobbin thread, leaving a zigzag thread on the back of your quilt. This may be appropriate for a wall quilt or smaller project, but has the potential of snagging and catching when used for larger quilts. Experiment with different width spacing in double needles to see what the outcome is.

THREADS

Quilters often give little thought to the purchase of thread, but it is very important to the longevity of a quilt. You should buy the highest quality thread available for all your sewing projects, but be especially careful when purchasing thread for your quilts.

Choose a thread that is not as strong as the fabric in your quilt top. I prefer 100% mercerized cotton for both piecing and quilting. Years from now, after much use and many launderings of a quilt, you will appreciate this choice of thread. It is possible to repair a quilting line where the thread has broken, but it is impossible to repair the fabric that has been "cut" by a thread that was stronger than the fabric.

Think of garments that you may have had that when extra stress was put on a seam, the fabric ripped. Chances are the thread was too strong and abrasive, and it wore down the fibers of the fabric.

Size 50, 3-ply cotton mercerized thread is recommended for all light to medium-weight cotton fabrics. Cotton thread is strong, smooth, lustrous, and resists shrinkage. Never buy bargain thread for machine sewing. It is usually made from short fibers, which make it weak and abrasive. Check the thread for long, staple fibers; it should not have a fuzzy appearance. If it is smooth, with very few fibers appearing, it is generally a high-quality thread. This applies to both cotton and polyester threads.

Use cotton-wrapped polyester thread only when using polyester blends in the quilt top and lining. It is too thick for cotton fabrics, and can cause puckered seams and abrasion.

The guidelines to help you in choosing threads are:

❖ Choose thread that is the same fiber type as the fabric you are sewing.

❖ Thread should be weaker than the fabric.

❖ Thread should be the same size as the threads weaving the fabric. Too thin of a thread will be too weak and can break easily under stress, and too coarse of a thread will wear prematurely, as it lays on the surface of the fabric and breaks down due to being exposed to constant abrasion.

Many quilters use 2-ply threads in their quilting. One thing to consider is that 2-ply threads are very weak. If stress and weight are applied to the quilt, these threads will generally not hold up to the abuse. The exception is when you are doing extremely close quilting, where the threads are stitched into the quilt close enough to support the weight sufficiently. Never use 2-ply embroidery threads if ditch quilting is the only quilting put into the quilt, or if quilting distances are spaced further apart than 1/2". Avoid pairing 2-ply threads with nylon. The nylon is stronger than they are, and has a tendency to cut them.

INVISIBLE NYLON

Invisible nylon is the only exception I make to the use of cotton threads in cotton quilts. But be very careful and critical of the quality you purchase. Use only the finest, highest quality nylon available. It is made strictly for artwork, not for sewing draperies and hems.

There is a vast difference in weights and qualities of nylon thread. The size needed is .004. I cannot stress how important it is that the proper brands of nylon thread are used in your quilts. The most recognized brands are Sew Art International invisible nylon and YLI Wonder Thread®. Be sure the label says .004. Try to break the thread. It should break very easily. It should not be at all course or stiff. Avoid buying nylon thread that comes on large cones, as the weight is slightly different from the small tubes, and the thread becomes brittle after it is stored on the cone for long periods. Failure to use the proper thread could result in broken stitches, torn fabric, and undue wear and tear to the quilt. Using the above-mentioned brands and sizes will result in years of pleasure and use from your quilts.

FIG. 2.6 Recommended nylon thread

Always try to buy and use fresh thread in smaller amounts. Look for thread packaged on 3"-long cardboard tubes or small white cones (about 2 1/2" tall), wrapped with cellophane (Figure 2.6). It should not be on a regular thread spool, or jump off the spool like a spring when the package is opened.

When you open the thread, run your fingers down a length of the thread. It should be as smooth and fine as a hair shaft. If it has a gritty or crimped feel, the thread has been overly stretched in the spooling process, and will tend to break and snarl, making the quilting process very frustrating. I advise returning the thread and replacing it with a smooth spool. Often when you are getting toward the end of a spool of nylon, the thread takes on the shape of the spool and starts to coil. When this happens, replace it with a fresh new spool. Your local quilt shop or machine arts store and many sewing machine dealers carry these products.

The nylon thread needs to be weaker than the bobbin thread. Regular nylon sewing thread is like fishing line and is very difficult to break. It also feels tough and coarse. If you use this thread and stress is applied to the quilt, the thread will tear the fabric and pop the bobbin thread. The soft invisible nylon thread, however, stretches with stress and works with the bobbin thread.

Invisible nylon is the only thread that gives machine quilting a hand-quilted appearance, especially when quilted with cotton thread in the bobbin. The softness of the cotton allows the stitch to bend and give a softer appearance to the stitch. NEVER use polyester thread in the bobbin with nylon thread. The abrasive polyester fibers will serrate the nylon, causing unsightly broken stitches; the polyester thread also gives a flat, stiff look to the stitches.

Invisible nylon is a continuous nylon filament that comes in a clear or smoke color. The clear thread is used on light-colored fabric; the smoke thread is used on darker fabrics. All that can be seen is the depression of the quilting line, not the thread itself. The thread takes on the color of each fabric it is sewn into. A regular cotton thread would be highly visible when crossing many colors of fabric, and would detract from the beauty of the quilt.

Although invisible nylon thread can be used either on the top or in the bobbin, I would limit its use in the bobbin. It tends to leave a stiff, harsh line of stitching, instead of the soft, up-and-down look of the cotton and nylon used together. I prefer to thread only the top of the machine with the nylon, and I use a 50 weight, 3-ply, 100% cotton sewing thread in the bobbin. The bobbin thread should match the lining fabric as closely as possible. This combination also eliminates snarling and breaking, which can be very frustrating when nylon is used for both top and bobbin. If you do choose to use the nylon thread on the bobbin, the winding procedure is different than for sewing threads. Do not insert the thread through the thread guides and tension regulators, as this causes the thread to stretch. Simply use your hand to guide the thread onto the bobbin as you run the machine.

You may loosen your machine tension on the top to allow for the weight difference of the two threads, and for the high thread drag and stretchiness of the nylon thread. A size 80/12 needle is recommended, but you may find that the needle hole is too large and that the nylon thread does not fill the hole. A size 70/10 or a 75/11 needle might be more appropriate for certain fabrics.

SPECIALTY THREADS

On one-color projects, such as whitework quilts, jackets, dresses, etc., the nylon might look too much like plastic when doing a lot of heavy quilting. In this case, try machine embroidery thread. This is a 2-ply, 100% cotton thread used for machine artwork. It is very fine and delicate, but should not be substituted for the heavier sewing-weight thread used with the nylon. The embroidery thread is used when a great deal of stitching is being put into the fabric. It sews into the fabric flatter than heavier threads, and it leaves a beautiful texture. DMC® and Swiss-Metrosene® both make machine embroidery threads. Look for size 50 or 60; 30 weight is usually too heavy.

As machine quilting becomes more popular, different threads are being used with great imagination. Don't overlook metallic and rayon threads to add sparkle and shine to your quilting. Experiment with different brands. Refer to the section in this chapter on needles to learn about special needles made for these threads. There are good and bad threads for quilting. Your experience and testing will guide you to those that will work success-fully in your machine. Brands to try include Sulky® rayon and metallic, Madeira® metallic, Natesh® rayon, and Kanagawa metallic.

When using any of the specialty threads—nylon, rayon, or metallic—avoid putting the spool on the spool pin of the machine. These threads tend to be slick and come off the ends of the spools easily. Instead, use a cone holder or small jar that will hold the spool upright and off the machine. Set the cone holder on the right side in back of the machine (Figure 2.8 point A). This keeps the thread from getting caught in the quilt. If you do not have some sort of thread guide on the back of your machine, guiding the thread at the same angle as the spool pins, use a closed safety pin taped to the spool pin base (Figure 2.8 point B). As you thread the machine, insert it through the small hole in the safety pin first, then through the normal threading procedure. This will make the thread track from the same direction it would have if it were on the spool pin itself. Some machines have a thread guide attach-ment for this area, or they have one built into the area. Use this instead of the safety pin if your machine is so equipped (Figure 2.7).

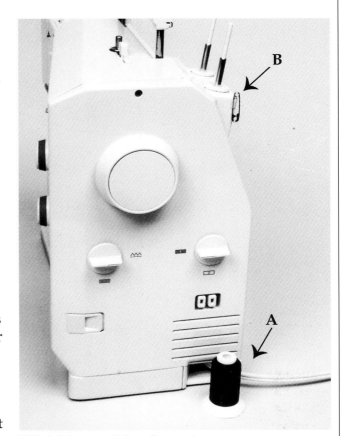

FIG. 2.8 Suggested threading system

If you do not have a cone holder, a small jar (like an olive jar) works well as long as the jar does not allow the spool to fall over on its side (Figure 2.7). The small white cones do not need a jar or cone holder. They simply sit on the table at the back of the machine. It must stand upright so the thread comes off from the top. Again, use the safety pin thread guide system.

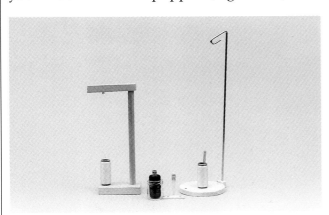

FIG. 2.7 Cone holders

HEIRLOOM
MACHINE
QUILTING

22

❖ PART TWO ❖

PREPARING THE QUILT

HEIRLOOM
MACHINE
QUILTING

24

CHOOSING A QUILT DESIGN

O nce the quilt top is complete, press it extremely well using moisture or a steam setting. Generally, you press the quilt top on the right side of the fabric. Press throughout the quilt piecing process to ensure a flat and true top when you are finished. Check the seam allowances to make sure that you do not have "accordions" in them. Accordions are little folds or pleats that get pressed in when pressing from the wrong side of the fabric during construction. These pleats create problems for you when machine quilting, especially ditch quilting. To avoid them, lay the piece on the ironing surface right side up. With the side of the iron, gently push the seam allowance to one side.

Once the quilt top is pressed smooth and flat, you are ready to mark the quilting patterns or lines onto its surface. If you are only ditch quilting, no marking is necessary. Not all quilting patterns and stencils are appropriate for beginning machine quilters. Continuous line patterns lend themselves easily to machine quilting. These patterns can be either simple or complicated in design, but their lines do not start and stop or weave in and out.

Look for patterns that you can finger trace. Start in one spot, and trace through the entire design without starting, stopping, or retracing any lines. Finger trace the designs in Figure 3.1.

Another example of continuous-line design would be the two feathers in Figure 3.2. The feather on the left is a traditional feather design. When hand quilting, it is easy to push the needle between the layers of the quilt to get from one spot to another, but this cannot be done with a sewing machine needle. There are two alternatives on the machine:

1 Lock off the threads at the beginning and end of every design line. This creates a sloppy looking back, and weakens the quilting

OR

2 Retrace the same line—exactly—to quilt the design and move from line to line without breaking the thread. Optimally this stitching is "in and out" in the same needle holes. This will take quite a bit of practice to achieve the accuracy needed.

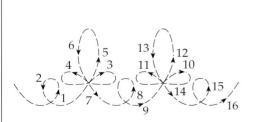
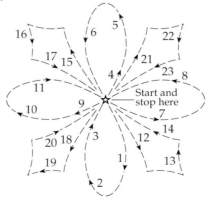
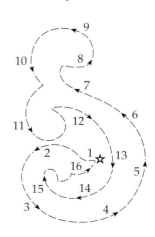

FIG. 3.1 Continuous quilting designs

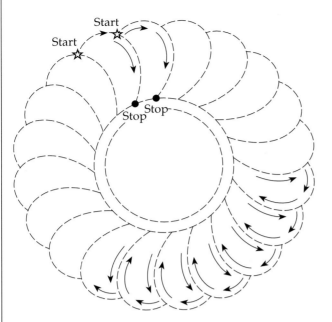

FIG. 3.2 Traditional and continuous feathered wreaths

The feather on the right can be worked continuously. Every petal has its own in-and-out stitching line, and you still can achieve a beautiful feather! You can master this design with very little practice.

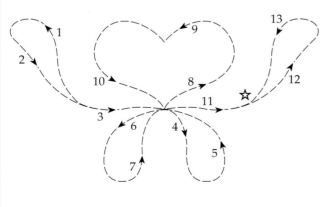

FIG. 3.3 Adapting designs to be continuous

Most designs you find will not be continuous. But you can often still work with them if you can find a way to turn them into a continuous line system. Finger trace the designs in Figure 3.3 and see how the non-continuous lines can be done on the machine.

Sources for quilting designs can be found everywhere: coloring books, greeting cards, advertisements, folk art books, cut paper designs, as well as precut stencils and over 20 titles of books devoted strictly to quilting patterns. Patterns are not normally available in the size you need. In the next section, I will discuss sizing the pattern to the quilt.

FIG. 3.4 Quilting design sources

QUILTING STENCILS

More and more continuous line stencils are becoming available, but every design you may want won't always be precut, and often the design is available, but not in the size that you need. Here are some tricks for making your own stencils any size you need. These are very simple and inexpensive, and will provide a wealth of designs to draw from. **Note:** if you have trouble finding any of these products, see page 176.

Your local printer can make the pattern the size you want with no trouble. Most copy shops have equipment that can enlarge or reduce the pattern without distortion. Once you get the pattern to the desired size, you have several options for making it usable.

DOUBLE-BLADED KNIFE METHOD

Many quilt shops carry DBK™ plastic. This is a very soft, clear plastic that is easily cut with an Exacto® knife. Use a double-bladed knife (also known as a Leaded Glass Pattern Cutter by Exacto) to cut the channels needed for the stencil. Begin by tracing the pattern lines onto the plastic with a permanent marker. Cut on either a rotary cutter mat or on a piece of glass. The knife cuts two parallel lines 1/8" apart, creating a channel. As you cut, lift the knife every so often to create the "bridges" necessary to keep the stencil from falling apart. After all the channels are cut, use a single-bladed knife or a small pair of scissors to clip out the ends of each channel. Now you have channel space for your marking device.

This method is especially useful for designs that have long, curvy lines where you can make a long, smooth cut. I have found that small, intricate patterns can be more difficult to cut with this method. After you have finished cutting the stencil, wipe off any permanent marker lines left on the plastic to avoid transferring ink onto your fabric.

FIG. 4.1 *Tracing onto plastic*

FIG. 4.2 *Cutting with double-bladed knife*

HOT PEN METHOD

Another fast method of making stencils involves using a hot pen. The instrument used is similar to a woodburning tool. **Note:** It is only safe to use this tool with Dupont Mylar®, not plastic. You will know Mylar by the hard finish and the brittle feel and sound. Plastics emit toxic fumes when melted that are dangerous to your health.

While the pen is plugged in and heating up, trace your design onto the Mylar with a permanent pen. You will need to curl the Mylar up and off the surface of the table to achieve a clean cut with the pen. The instructions tell you to burn the Mylar on a piece of glass, but the channel does not melt through clean. I have found it much more satisfactory to curl it up and work off the surface. Rest your forearm against the table to steady your hand. Insert the hot pen tip into the Mylar at the beginning of a line. Slowly and evenly follow the line with the hot tip. When you need to stop for a bridge, pull the pen tip out straight, leave a space, then continue cutting.

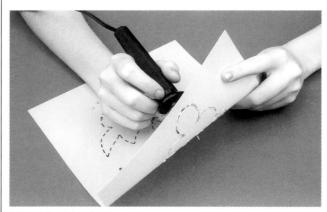

FIG. 4.3 *Using hot pen*

This tool is very helpful in making small, intricate patterns. Remove the bumps on the back of the stencil with a sanding block or a single-edge razor blade.

Both methods make durable, long-lasting stencils. Plan your cuts so that you get the longest line possible to speed your marking time. Long, straight, or wavy lines can be cut up to 2½" before allowing for a bridge. Smaller areas and circles should have cuts of only ½"-1" between bridges. Leave sufficient bridges to keep the stencil sturdy.

TULLE METHOD

If you need a design quickly and for short-term use, bridal illusion, tulle, is an option. This very fine, soft netting is used to make wedding veils and is readily available at fabric stores.

To use, lay the tulle on top of the copy of your design and pin. Trace the design onto the tulle using a permanent black felt-tip marker like a Sharpie® or a laundry marker. To prevent any residue from the marker from going onto the quilt when marking the quilt top, rinse the tulle out in soapy water. Press with a warm iron to dry.

FIG. 4.4 *Tracing onto tulle*

Place the tulle on the quilt top, pin in place, and use a liquid fabric marker, such as the water-soluble Mark-B-Gone™ or an air erasable pen to transfer your pattern. (A liquid marker is preferable.) As you are tracing the lines on the tulle, the liquid ink goes into the holes of the tulle and leaves dots on your quilt top, marking your quilting line. When the tulle is removed, the entire pattern is on the top, ready to quilt.

FIG. 4.5 *Tracing through tulle onto quilt top*

This is a very simple and practical way to mark designs without having any bridges. You do not need to guess where the line should be at the bridges. However, water-soluble marking tools do not work on dark fabrics, dry pencils tend to tear the tulle, and chalk powders brush off too easily.

TEAR-AWAY METHOD

There is an alternate method for marking problem fabrics such as velvet, lamé, satins, sateens, silks, etc. Use Tear-Away, a very soft, paper-type product that tears cleanly away from stitching. If you are doing a large project, sew pieces of Tear-Away together to get the needed size. This method can be used on very small areas like pockets on velvet jackets, or it can be used on large projects like whole-cloth quilts.

FIG. 4.6 Tear-Away method

Mark your pattern onto the Tear-Away. When putting the quilt layers together, position the Tear-Away over the quilt top, so you have four layers to your sandwich. Then quilt through all four layers. After quilting, gently remove the Tear-Away from the stitching. This is not a speed technique, just a safe one that protects fragile fabrics. Tear-Away comes in either soft or crisp. EZ Notions has taken this method and developed a paper product that works in the same manner called Stitch Thru™. This paper comes in blank sheets as well as several pre-printed patterns ready for use

RUG-CANVAS METHOD

Cross-hatch quilting is very attractive and can usually be done easily on the machine. However, it is not easy to mark on the quilt top. Use a latch-hook rug canvas to make your stencil. Because it is an even-weave fabric, there are squares woven in. By marking permanent lines in a grid on the canvas, you automatically have a perfect grid. (Use a permanent ink felt-tip marker such as the Sharpie.) Follow the squares in a straight line to keep the line straight and the angle accurate.

By counting the number of holes between each line, you can keep the spacing consistent. Mark the grid lines as far apart as you like. The grid can be diagonal, straight, double diagonal, one straight and one diagonal, etc.

FIG. 4.7 Marking grid onto rug canvas

To mark the quilt top, place the canvas on the quilt in the proper position and pin if necessary. Using a felt-tip fabric marker, such as Mark-B-Gone, start with one line and make a dot with the marker in the hole that the line goes through. Continue doing this up the length of the line. Now come back down on the next line, making a dot in each hole you come to along the line. Do all of one direction first, then repeat the process for the other direction. When the canvas is removed, you will have dotted lines that are perfect in spacing as well as angle.

Rug canvas, available at craft stores that sell latch-hook rug supplies, comes by the yard so you can make your stencil any size you need. For borders, the canvas can be cut the width of the border, in an "L" shape to accommodate the corner and half of the length of each side border. This way you only need to align the canvas four times, and the corners are marked perfectly. Rug canvas stencils can be used many times.

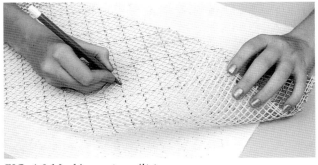

FIG. 4.8 Marking onto quilt top

LIGHT BOX

Another alternative to cutting stencils is the use of a light box for tracing. This method is especially useful for large projects where much time would be needed to prepare stencils or where the quilting pattern is very detailed.

You can set up a light box system inexpensively by using a lamp and a table that expands. Expand the table to create an opening, and cover the open area with a sheet of glass. Place a lamp without the shade on the floor below the glass. Higher wattage bulbs make it easier to trace onto dark fabrics.

Trace your quilting pattern onto white butcher paper using a bold black line. Tape the pattern onto the glass. Turn the lamp on, allowing the light to shine through the glass and paper. Position the quilt top over the paper. The fabric becomes translucent, enabling you to see through the fabric to the marked lines. Trace the lines onto the quilt top, repositioning when necessary.

FIG. 4.9 Light box

PIN-PRICK METHOD

Antique quilts are excellent sources for quilting designs, often originals not readily found elsewhere. To copy a pattern from an antique quilt, place a sheet of butcher paper over cardboard, cork, or carpeting. Lay the antique quilt on top of the paper. With a sharp pin or needle, prick through the quilt and the paper as you follow the quilting lines. This method of transferring the pattern causes minimal damage to the quilt and eliminates the risk of making lines on the quilt by surface tracing.

FIG. 4.10 Pin pricking to obtain design

SIZING A QUILTING DESIGN TO FIT A BORDER

Border stencils and patterns seldom automatically fit within the borders of a quilt. There is a simple mathematical way to figure the adjustments needed to make a design fit a given area. Work through the following example using a quilt that measures 84" by 96". Figure each side separately. Carefully measure the finished edge of one side of your quilt. For this example use the 96" side.

1 Measure your quilting design from the outermost corner to the beginning of the first pattern repeat (Figure 4.11a). Make a note of this measurement. This example measures 4.75".

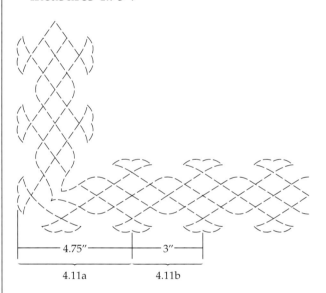

|← 4.75" →|← 3" →|

4.11a   4.11b

FIG. 4.11a Measurement of outermost corner
FIG. 4.11b Measurement of pattern repeat

2 Double that measurement to accommodate both corners of that side.
Example: 4.75" + 4.75" = 9.5"

3 Subtract the amount in Step 2 from the border length.
Example: 96" - 9.5" = 86.5"

4 Into this measurement, divide the length of one pattern repeat (Figure 4.11b).

Example: $\frac{86.5"}{3"} = 28.83$

This number tells you how many repeats are needed to fill the border space.

Note: You will need to decide whether it would be easier to shorten or lengthen the design when the answer is not a round number. In this example, it would be easier to round up to 29 repeats.

5 Multiply the pattern repeat measurement by the number of repeats needed.
Example: 29 repeats X 3" = 87"

6 Using the two measurements that you got from Steps 3 and 5, subtract the smaller from the larger. If Step 3 is larger, the pattern repeat will need to be lengthened. If Step 5 is larger, the pattern repeat will need to be shortened.
Example: 87" - 86.5" = .5"

7 Divide the answer from Step 6 by the number of repeats needed for the border. This number tells you how much adjustment needs to be made to each pattern repeat.

Example: $\frac{.5"}{29"} = .017$

In this example, each pattern repeat will need to be made shorter by .017 inches. This adjustment can be made on the stencil if you are cutting your own, or on the quilt as you mark the pattern.

PREPARING THE QUILT FOR MARKING

Registration lines, used for placement accuracy, need to be marked onto the quilt's surface before marking any designs. Precut stencils are not always straight on the plastic so it is up to you to determine the actual size of the design and how it should sit on the quilt. The size you need to determine is the actual area of the design itself, not the plastic.

BLOCK OR FILL DESIGNS

For block stencils, you need to find the exact center of the pattern, as well as the center points on the outside edges of the design. See Figure 4.12. Measure the quilt block so that you know where the center points of the block are, both in the middle of the square and on the outside edges. See Figure 4.13. Align the stencil registration lines with the markings on the block. This will assure a centered and well-placed design.

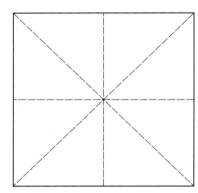

FIG. 4.12 Registration lines for quilt block

FIG. 4.13 Registration lines for stencil

BORDERS AND CORNERS

Below are instructions for setting the registration lines on the border and in the corners. Chapter 5 tells which marking tools to use.

1 Mark a 45° angle line in each corner.

FIG. 4.14 Diagonal corner registration lines

2 If there are no seams, draw a line with a ruler that extends the border seamlines across the width of the border on all sides.

FIG. 4.15 Corner registration lines

3 Find the midpoint of the border width. Measure from the corner of the quilt top (the border seam) to the edge of the border.

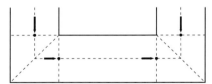

FIG. 4.16 Finding midpoints

Subtract the $1/4$" seam allowance from this measurement. Mark a dot at each corner on the lines drawn in the previous step. Connect the width midpoints with a line the length of each border.

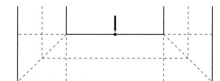

FIG. 4.17 Finding border length midpoint

4 Measure the length of each border to find the
    midpoint. Make a mark on the border seam.

PREPARING THE STENCIL

Mark the registration lines directly onto the stencil with a permanent pen.

1 Draw a line to show the 45° angle of the corner.

2 Find the center of the design and draw a line the length of the stencil.

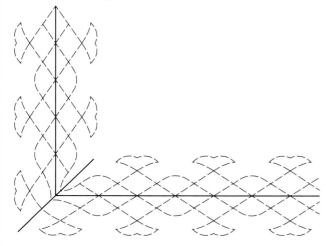

FIG. 4.18 *Registration marks on border stencil*

These lines will lie directly on top of the quilt registration lines. By having the register set, the stencils will always line up with the borders and turn the corners accurately.

When all the register lines are set, you will be ready to mark the quilt top. The next chapter will help you choose marking pencils and pens for your quilts.

MARKING TOOLS

There are many marking tools available and it is the quilter's responsibility to make sure that the marker chosen is safe for the fabric used. Consumers need to be aware that while the marking tools say "quilter's," or is endorsed by a well-known quilter, it is not a guarantee that the pencil is safe to use under all conditions. What works perfectly for one quilter may be disastrous for another. Several different markers may be needed on a single quilt, because different fabrics in the quilt will react differently to the same marker. Also consider what method you use to remove the marked lines.

MARKING PENCILS

Traditionally, a graphite pencil has been used to draw directly onto the quilt top. Do not use a #2 soft lead pencil because the cotton fabric tends to absorb the line and seldom releases it totally. A #4H hard lead engineering pencil works well. The point stays sharp and leaves a very light line. It is suitable for light solids, muslin, and white fabrics. Some hard-lead mechanical pencils are excellent choices, as they remain sharp.

There are a variety of markers available for light and print fabrics. Below I have listed those that are satisfactory for machine quilting. Not all pencils used by hand quilters are successful for machine work. Remember that while machine quilting, you are subject to working with shadows and inadequate lighting. You will also be quilting fairly fast. You will need a marker that will give you a bold line that is easy to see, but also easy to remove.

A brand that gives excellent results is Caran D'Ache's Supracolor® I. These are watercolor pencils that are easily removed from fabric, but the only colors that I would use are white, gold, and silver. Do not use the other colors, as the pigment can cause problems. These pencils leave a dark, bold line. Use a very light touch so the lead is not ground into the fabric. Marks wipe off easily with a damp cloth. Dixon Washout Cloth Markers are very good for prints and colors. They are available in red, green, and blue. The red and green are especially helpful when marking on darker prints.

A word of warning about the chalk wheels that have been so popular in the past few years. In many cases the dye in the chalk does not wash out of the fabric or the thread. Always test the red, blue, and yellow chalks. Yellow can be especially troublesome because the sulfur in it tends to be permanent in fabrics. The white has no dye, so it is perfectly safe.

There are several good white markers that can be used on dark fabrics. A white charcoal pencil called Charcoal White®, from General Pencil Co. is very good, as is the white pastel pencil from Germany called Carb-Othello®. Neither of these has additives that can cause problems on fabrics. Be careful about using white dressmaker's chalk pencils because their high wax content makes the lines difficult to remove. They are made to mark on the inside of garments, not on the right side.

New marking products are always being found for use on quilts. General Pencil Co. has pencils new to quilters, the Multi-Pastel Chalks®, that work very well, as does the new Berol Karismacolor® Graphite Aquarelle®, which is a water-soluble graphite pencil. I've found the medium lead to work best. Keep an eye out for other new products that would be applicable to your quilting needs.

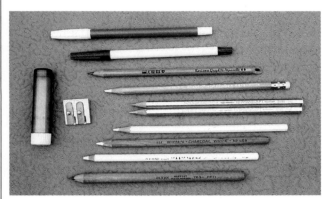

FIG. 5.1 Various marking pencils

Always pretest all marking devices you have chosen before marking the quilt top. Because of the variety of sizings and finishes on fabrics, as well as dye properties, each fabric can react differently to various marking tools. A pencil may be safe on every fabric in the quilt except one, but you won't know that until it has ruined that fabric. Never take anyone's word for the reliability of a marking tool on your fabric.

The test is simple and should be done whether you prewash the fabrics or not. Gather scraps of every fabric in the quilt that you need to mark. Have a variety of marking tools that will show on each fabric color. Mark lines on each scrap, making the line as dark as you need to see it readily.

Note: This is where machine quilters can get into trouble with marking tools. Hand quilters can work with very faint lines, because they generally have good light and no vision obstructions. The machine, however, has a poor lighting system, leaving us with shadows and dark spots. We also have limited vision because of the machine head. This makes it necessary to have darker lines. Making dark lines by pressing hard with any pencil can spell trouble!

Once you have the lines marked, take a damp cloth and rub gently with the grain of the fabric to remove the lines. If the lines come off easily, the marking tool is a good choice for that one particular fabric. Do this test with each fabric sample. You may need a variety of tools for marking the various fabrics in your quilt top.

Some pencils do not come off easily but can be removed when laundering. If you plan to launder the quilt, pretest the markers either when you prewash the fabrics or by using soapy water on your samples. Avoid using fabric erasers, as they will lift a nap on the fabric and leave unsightly damage. Also be careful of chemicals, as they may cause a color to run and ruin the quilt.

Graphite pencil lines can be removed by applying the following mixture to the line and rubbing gently with a soft toothbrush. Follow by wiping with a cloth and then laundering.

❖ *1 part water*

❖ *3 parts rubbing alcohol*

❖ *1-2 drops Palmolive™ or Joy™ dishwashing soap (do not use Dawn™)*

WASH-OUT LIQUID MARKING PENS

Felt-tip liquid markers used in quiltmaking have received a lot of bad publicity. These are better known as Mark-B-Gone™, FadeAway™, etc. They usually have blue or purple ink that is removable with water. They are now available in white for use on dark fabrics.

When they first appeared on the market, they were "miracle" markers, but time has shown them to be potentially dangerous to fabric unless used properly. These pens were developed for dressmaking, and instructions were not originally included. Quilters began using them without thoroughly removing them, causing the lines to discolor and become permanent. The chemical, if left in the fabric, weakens and breaks down the fibers.

The lines can be heat set and become permanent if ironed or exposed to high heat while in the fabric. Be especially careful of the purple air-erasable pens. Strong light and humidity make these lines totally disappear. However, the chemical still in the fabric causes permanent and unsightly damage to the quilt if not removed thoroughly. Remove the chemical after the quilting is finished. Completely submerge the quilt into cold, clear water. Do not use soaps or detergents because their ingredients can also set the lines. Soak the quilt until all the lines have totally disappeared. Then launder it in a neutral detergent such as Orvus Paste® and warm water to remove the chemical from the fibers. Once this has been done, you will not have a problem with the felt-tip pens.

To pretest, mark the lines onto scraps of the designated fabrics. I do this as I cut the fabrics for the quilt. I find that it takes me as long to piece and appliqué as to quilt, so the ink is in the fabric under similar conditions.

Once the top is finished, take the samples and soak in cool, clear water until the lines disappear, then wash in soapy water. Rinse, then iron dry with a hot iron. If the lines do not reappear in any way, you are safe with that fabric. If the lines reappear when ironed, the fibers have not released the chemical, and there is a potential for damage.

Visit your local quilt shop, craft supply store, or art supply store for a good selection of marking pencils and pens. Try a variety of tools and pretest them all before marking your quilt top.

BATTING—
THE INSIDE STORY

One of the most overlooked, least understood, and least discussed products in quiltmaking is batting. This key ingredient can either enhance a quilt's beauty or detract from, and distort, the quilt's surface. No one batting is appropriate for every quilt. Quilters must consider factors such as desired surface texture, weight, warmth, loft, drape, shrinkage, fiber content, washability, and wearability, bearding properties, ease of needling, etc. All of these factors play as important a role in the quilt's overall appearance as do fabric choices, design piecing, and the appliqué techniques. Remember, a top is not a quilt until it is quilted, and batting makes the quilt a quilt.

Machine quilting adds another dimension to your batting choices. As a beginner, you want to use a batting that will cooperate with you and your machine to eliminate distortion and thus frustration. As your skills improve, so does your willingness to take on more unruly battings. The fiber content, manufacturing process, and loft of each different batting will affect the manageability and success of the quilting process.

There are many excellent batttings on the market, but there is no one perfect batt. I will enumerate the products available and tell you the pros and cons of each. I will divide the batting products by fiber content and give you guidelines on spacing the quilting lines, and laundering. Keep in mind that machine quilting techniques are very different from hand quilting techniques. Battings that are difficult to hand needle are suddenly excellent choices for the machine.

When I lecture about battings in the classroom, I have many quilts to use for visual examples of each batting. That visual stimulation is not possible in a book. After you have read through the following information on each batting, I strongly suggest you take the time to do the samples and run the tests I give later in this chapter. The information given will make more sense and be more relevant to your particular tastes and style of quilting if you have the products in front of you to see, feel, and experiment with.

NATURAL FIBERS

The most commonly used natural fibers in quiltmaking are cotton and wool. Research and development in the United States has brought us excellent new, natural fiber products for use in quilts, including the blending of small amounts of polyester with cotton. With some basic understanding of the fibers and their characteristics and behaviors, you can enjoy using these battings in your quilts with excellent results. And, as evidenced by our antique quilts, natural fibers stand the test of time.

COTTON

Cotton battings were first manufactured in the 1850s, and today's battings are similarly manufactured. Harvested cotton bolls are sent through a cotton gin to separate the cotton fibers from the seed. This process also removes foreign matter such as dirt, twigs, leaves, and parts of the bolls. Next, the result-ing fiber, or cotton lint, is packed into large bales and sent to a spinning mill. At the mill, the cotton is opened to remove any remaining impurities. This process consists of a beating mechanism that loosens the cotton. The opened fibers are blown against a perforated drum, and the impurities are removed. The shorter fibers also pass through the drum, leaving the longer fibers to be rolled into a sheet. The result of this process is what we use for batting. It is finished with a glazing or resin to help prevent shifting and lumping.

When I began teaching machine quilting nationally in 1986, there were only two cotton battings available: Mountain Mist® 100% Natural and Fairfield Cotton Classic®. I was a true advocate of cotton because its characteristics lend itself to machine quilters, especially beginners. As more and more quilters learned about cotton, the demand for cotton battings increased. Manufacturer's created new, innovative products that lent themselves to the needs of today's quilters. Where there were only two major companies making two different battings, now there are numerous types and thicknesses available. There seems to be a cotton batting to fill the needs of most every type of quilter. Listed below are characteristics of cotton that accommodate the needs of machine quilters:

❖ The cotton fibers of the batting stick to the quilt top and backing fabrics, preventing the shifting, slipping, distortion, and stretching that occur with polyester battings under the machine. This allows us to pin baste less, and eliminates puckers, tucks, and ruffled borders on our machine-quilted quilts. This is the major reason for a beginning machine quilter to use cotton battings.

❖ Because the fibers do stick together and the batting is much thinner, when the quilt is rolled to go through the sewing machine, the roll is much smaller.

❖ Now king-sized, cotton-batted quilts can be quilted in one piece. The roll stays rolled while going through the machine, and takes up much less space.

FIG. 6.1 100% cotton battings

❖ Most cotton battings shrink some when washed. The shrinkage is generally at the same rate or higher than the cotton fabrics used in the quilt. (Avoid using fabric blends with cotton batting because the quilt fabric and the batt can shrink at very different rates.) Shrinkage can be beneficial for several reasons. It gives the quilt an aged look, which is desirable when trying to replicate an antique quilt. Also, when you are just learning to machine quilt, there are glitches in your work that you want to camouflage. The shrinkage of the batting, when the quilt is first laundered, causes puckering around the stitching. This makes it difficult to tell how the quilt was quilted, and hides many of the little problem areas. This way, you can learn to machine quilt on quilts, instead of wasting hours of precious time on muslin samples.

❖ Cotton is extremely comfortable to sleep under. Cotton breathes, allowing excess heat to escape. Thus you are never too hot under cotton quilts. For this reason, it is excellent for baby quilts. Quilts with cotton batts are not quite as warm as polyester or wool, but for many, polyester and wool are too hot. Cotton is also less dangerous around heat sources, as it is not combustible and does not melt like polyester. It can also be sanitized.

❖ Cotton endures. Even with hard use, cotton ages gracefully, becoming softer and more cuddly with age.

❖ Pure cotton battings do not beard like polyester battings. The fibers that do come through the fabric break off at the surface and blow off like a powder.

MOUNTAIN MIST® 100% NATURAL COTTON

Mountain Mist has been producing this batting, or one very similar, for more than 100 years. This batting is the only one on the market that gives quilts an antique appearance of softness and puckering most characteristic of the quilts from the 1900s to the 1930s. It is appropriate for the quilt tops made from the marvelous reproduction fabrics of that era. If you put polyester batting into these quilt tops, they do not look old, but fluffy and smooth instead. The batting choices you make are critical to the look and authenticity of the finished product. 100% Natural is made from cotton lint. It has to be quilted no farther apart than 1". The package suggests $1/4$"-$1/2$" spacing. That is a tremendous amount of quilting by hand, but it only takes a matter of hours for the machine quilter. Remember, you can machine quilt every $1/2$" faster than you can hand quilt every 6". Most hand quilters dislike this batting because it tends to be hard to needle. The machine needle has the opposite reaction. It can penetrate almost anything, so the density of the fibers is not an issue. Because the batting and fabric stick together, the machine presser foot does not feel any resistance or drag from the batting. It is able to glide over the fabric and designs more easily than when polyester batting is used. Because of this, I strongly suggest that you use this batting for your first larger project, and your success rate will climb.

100% Natural will shrink more than the other cotton products, often up to 2" in length and width when the quilt is washed and dried. It is not finished with any chemicals to bond it together — a natural starch is used to secure the fibers together for ease in handling. The starch will wash away when the quilt is laundered, so do not presoak this batting! Because you cannot pre-shrink this product, it is necessary to work with only non-washed fabrics. If you were to use this batting in prewashed quilt tops, when washed, the batting would shrink and the fabric would not, leaving the top too large for the batting. This can be unsightly for the quilt.

When considering the use of this batting, it should be for the soft look of the 1930's quilts puckered surface. If this is not the look you are seeking, consider using a different batting. There are many others that might fit your needs better. If you do choose to use prewashed fabrics, the shrinkage of the batting after washing can cause the batting to split and tear within the quilting lines. Closer quilting (1/4") may alleviate this.

To counteract the size loss and still get the look and feel you desire, you will need to make the quilt top larger. This is achieved by working with the samples at the end of this chapter and calculating the batting's percent of shrinkage. Make the quilt top that percentage larger. When this exercise is done, you will be able to have the quilt look like you want, and still fit the bed.

After reading through this entire book, practice the quilting techniques then make your first machine-quilted quilt out of non-washed, busy prints in medium- and dark-value fabrics, with 100% Natural batting and a very busy print backing. Quilt it, then wash and dry it. The medium and dark colors will camouflage the thread, and the puckering of the batting and fabric will camouflage the glitches that are a natural part of learning to machine quilt. Once the quilt is done, instead of criticizing your workmanship, put the quilt on your bed and sleep under it. You will find it extremely comfortable, and will soon not care that it is not "perfect." Please understand that I am not promoting poor-quality machine quilting. As adults, we want to take a class or read a book and become instant experts. This is not the case with machine quilting. It takes a lot of practice to master the skill. The best way to learn it is to make actual quilts and learn as you produce. Your first quilts will not be ribbon winners, but they will certainly keep you warm and comfortable. This batting gives you the permission to LEARN to machine quilt.

MOUNTAIN MIST® BLUE RIBBON

Blue Ribbon was developed by Mountain Mist as a result of consumer complaints about 100% Natural. Quilters expressed concern about how close Natural had to be quilted, how hard it was to hand needle, and the shrinkage rate was intolerable. What quilters requested was a batting with the softness and comfort of cotton but easier to hand quilt, could be quilted farther apart, and have minimal shrinkage. To be able to achieve these criteria, Mountain Mist made the batting from 100% cotton lint, with a bonding agent applied to the fiber for stability and strength. This process creates a 100% cotton fiber batting that shrinks very little, but can be quilted twice the distance as 100% Natural, up to 2" apart. To know how much shrinkage you can expect, run the tests given at the end of the chapter. Blue Ribbon has a thinner and flatter appearance than 100% Natural. It is not a substitute for 100% Natural; it's an alternative.

Blue Ribbon can be quilted at 1½"-2" intervals instead of 1" or closer. This allows you to use a cotton batting in a quilt that you do not wish to quilt so heavily, while retaining the comfort and beauty of cotton. It is equally easy to work with on the machine. You will not get the advantage of puckering when washed, even with unwashed fabrics. However, if you prefer to work with only prewashed fabrics or if you have an extensive collection of prewashed fabrics, you can now use a pure cotton batting with them. Blue Ribbon will not tear or split when laundered if quilting distances are within given guidelines. Again, do not presoak this batting!

Both 100% Natural and Blue Ribbon break down as a powder, eliminating bearding. They are both excellent choices for working with black or other dark fabrics where bearding is unsightly.

HEARTS OF THE WEST

Machine pieced, appliquéd, and quilted by Marla Yeager, Spokane, WA
using trapunto, free-motion, and stipple quilting techniques; nylon thread;
Hobbs Heirloom® premium cotton batting
86" x 103"

BALTIMORE-ALBUM STYLE FRIENDSHIP QUILT

Machine quilted by Barbara Alpan, Springfield, IL using blanket stitch and stipple quilting techniques; cotton thread; Hobbs Poly-Down® batting
70" x 70"

SCRAP NINE-PATCH

Reproduction of a quilt by Jean Wilbur, Columbia Cross Roads, PA; machine pieced and quilted by Harriet Hargrave using various free-motion techniques; nylon thread; Mountain Mist® 100% cotton batting
60" x 72"

PILGRIM'S PROGRESS

*Machine pieced and quilted by Harriet Hargrave using continuous curve, ditch,
and line quilting techniques; combination of nylon and cotton thread;
Hobbs Heirloom® premium 100% wool batting
69" x 69"*

A TOUCH OF AUTUMN

*Machine quilted by
Jean Lohmar, Galesburg, IL
using free-motion quilting;
nylon and cotton thread
25" x 26"*

GOLDEN FEATHERS

*Machine quilted by Jean Lohmar,
Galesburg, IL using free-motion
quilting; nylon and metallic thread
25" x 29"*

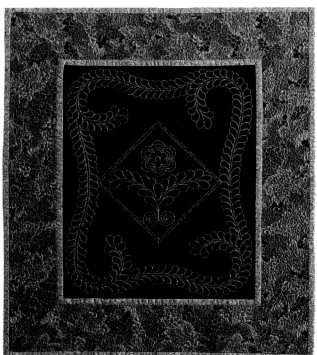

FEATHERED STAR

Machine pieced and quilted by Diane Gaudynski, Waukesha, WI using free-motion, straight line, and grid quilting techniques; nylon thread; Fairfield Cotton Classic® batting 80" x 95"

DOGWOOD

Machine embroidered, pieced, and quilted by Marla Yeager, Spokane, WA using free-motion quilting; cotton thread; Hobbs Heirloom® premium cotton batting 15" x 17"

PRIMROSE STAR

*Adapted from a 1925 quilt made by Bonnie Irwin Carden;
machine pieced by Nancy Hieronymus Barrett, Edmond, OK;
machine quilted by Harriet Hargrave using free-motion
quilting; DMC 50/2 machine embroidery thread;
Hobbs Heirloom® premium cotton batting
85" x 102"*

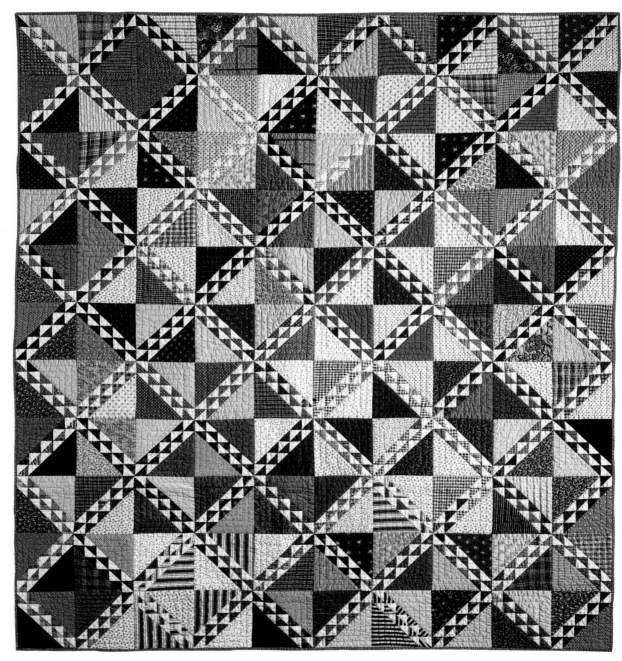

LONDON SQUARE

*Machine pieced by Harriet Hargrave; machine quilted by Barbara Trumbo using straight line
and ditch quilting techniques; nylon thread; Hobbs Heirloom® premium cotton batting
70" x 85"*

NEW GENERATION BATTINGS

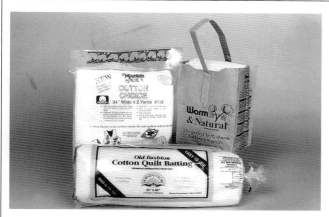

FIG. 6.2 *New generation battings*

A new type of batting has surfaced in the quilting world that takes cotton to a new dimension. Quilters have gotten in touch with the beauty and comfort of cotton fibers, but still complain about the heavy quilting needed on a loose-fiber batting.

Several companies have started to manufacture cotton products that are needle punched and stabilized, creating a cotton-felt type of product. These battings are allowing very distant quilting and great stability for hanging without distortion, but care must be taken in deciding where they are used.

At the time of this writing, the following felted battings are available: Morning Glory Old Fashioned™, Warm Products Inc. Warm and Natural™, and Mountain Mist Cotton Choice™. These battings are made from 100% cotton lint fibers, but are covered with a scrim before finishing. This is a thin sheet of polyester stabilizer that is placed on one side of the fiber web and then needle punched into the surface of the batt. This scrim keeps the fibers from stretching and distorting. It also keeps it from being as soft and drapeable as other battings. Needle punching is a process in which sheets of barbed needles come into contact with the fiber web, then compress and intertangle the fibers for stability. When the barb collapses, the needles are withdrawn. This is how felting occurs. These batts tend to leave the finished product much flatter and stiffer than the loose fiber batts. A resin finish is applied at the end.

These battings can be quilted up to 8" apart. There are important issues to be taken into consideration when contemplating quilting this far apart. If the quilt or wallhanging is not going to be laundered, this may not be a problem. However, if you will be washing the item often, the weight of the wet batting and fabric pulls against the sparse amount of quilting, causing damage to the stitches, as well as the fabric in the seams not supported by quilting. Great distances between quilting lines do not contribute to a healthy, long-lived quilt, but quilting closer, say 1"–2" apart, can cause the batting to become very stiff and flat. These battings may need to be relegated to wallhangings, craft projects, placemats, tablecloths, etc., where durability and firmness is desired, and not used in bed quilts, where softness and drapeability is needed. These battings can be prewashed, but this may not be needed. Some of them contain seed hulls, which have oil in them. This oil can bleed into and stain light-colored fabrics. Care must be taken to test these battings or they may permanently damage your quilt. Any batting with "trash" in it—leaf and stem particles—should be checked before using.

Some of these battings will shrink more than others. Again, if shrinkage is desired, test them to see what effect the shrinkage has on size loss and appearance.

Morning Glory also produces two battings that are 100% cotton fibers and are needle punched, but do not have the scrim attached to the surface. These are called Clearly Bleached (a pure white fiber batt) and Clearly Unbleached (a batt that uses natural-color fibers that still have leaves and stems, and possibly seed hull chips, left in). These two batts are very soft and drapeable because the scrim has been left off. It is rather stretchy because of this and might not be the best choice for wallhangings (where stretching could cause distortion). It is purported the quilting can be 4"–6" apart. This batting is more suitable for bed quilts.

COTTON FLANNEL

Flannel was very popular in antique quilts. Exquisite tiny hand stitches were made possible by the thinness of the cloth. Often overlooked today, cotton flannel yardage or flannel bed sheets are an excellent batting to be used in summer-weight quilts.

Flannelette is brushed on both sides, making it thicker. Because flannel is a woven fabric, as opposed to the non-woven fibers of batting, quilting distances can be even greater. Consider using flannel in baby quilts, lap robes, garments, wall quilts, etc. It can be used either as a batting or the back and batting all in one.

When purchasing flannel, look for a heavy thread count—no less than 68 threads per square inch. This will allow for the thickness that you will need, and prevent the severe shrinkage that is inherent to low thread count flannel. Do not purchase pajama flannels, as they are of very low thread count; shrinkage will be very high, plus they lack brushing and nap, which gives the heavier flannels density and thickness. The brushing is what makes it so good for use as a batting. A flannel called "loggers flannel" is a very heavy flannel where the nap does not pill, even after several washings. It is worth looking for.

COTTON/POLYESTER BLENDED BATTINGS

FIG. 6.3 *Cotton/polyester blended battings*

FAIRFIELD PROCESSING CORPORATION COTTON CLASSIC®

Cotton Classic is not a pure 100% cotton batting. It is made from blending 80% cotton lint fibers with 20% polyester fibers, forming a web, and bonding the web with a resin to keep the fibers together. This batting is similar to, yet very different, from the Mountain Mist cottons.

The resin on this batting can have a very grainy, rough feel. This seems objectionable to many quilters. This is not troublesome to the machine quilter, but it can make hand quilting very difficult. Fairfield recommends presoaking if you want to soften the batting to ease needling. Cotton Classic is hard to hand needle without presoaking, but it is not necessary to presoak for machine work, except when shrinkage is a consideration. Sometimes the batting will shrink, other times it will not, so you should do a shrinkage test on every new batt you purchase. Then, if you want shrinkage to be a part of your quilt's appearance and the batt you have tested doesn't shrink, you can substitute one that will, and not be disappointed. On the other hand, if you make a garment or quilt, and shrinkage is not desirable, you can presoak the batting.

Cotton Classic can be quilted at 2"-3" intervals. This allows you to use a cotton lint-type batting in items that before couldn't handle cotton because of the close quilting requirements. This batting is excellent in garments, as it breathes and adds no bulk or puff. One drawback is that it does have the potential to beard on black and dark fabrics.

Cotton Classic is soft, thin, and drapes beautifully, but still allows you to quilt up to 3" apart. On the other hand, it is one of the few battings that will let you quilt every $1/8$"– $1/4$" (an example is the quilt on page 121.) It will still be drapeable. You will find that after washing a quilt quilted extremely close, the areas that are not so heavily quilted will take on a puffy, or slightly raised appearance, giving a look similar to trapunto.

To presoak the batting, fill the washer with tepid water (no detergent or soap), unfold the batting, and gently push it into the water. Do not agitate. Let the batt rest in the water for 5 to 10 minutes, then spin the water out using the gentle spin cycle. Dry in the dryer on air or fluff for 15 to 20 minutes, until just dry. If it is necessary for you to use heat to get it dry, keep it on the lowest setting. Handle the batt carefully during this process. Cotton Classic has an antique, soft, textured appearance if used with new fabric without prewashing the batt.

HOBBS HEIRLOOM® PREMIUM COTTON

This batting is a direct result of the machine-quilting classes I teach. When we discuss the various cotton battings available, we inevitably discuss the desire for a batting that gives the look of 100% Natural, but does not require such close quilting; one that can be used with prewashed fabrics, not just new ones. Quilters want to be able to quilt 3" apart, and not only by machine but by hand. They want the comfort of cotton, but also the ease and lesser need of quilting they get with polyester. When no shrinkage is desired, the batting needs to be preshrunk. This is a lot to ask of one batt, and up until Heirloom, there was no batt that filled this criteria.

Heirloom was created to give the quilter the above characteristics, all in one batt. Instead of making the batt from short lint fibers, the batting is produced using a long staple cotton fiber. In order to manufacture it, and to stabilize it, a small percentage of polyester is added. Then the batting is very lightly needle punched, and lightly resinated with a soft resin. This leaves us with a batt that can be quilted 3"-4" apart. It will shrink slightly in unwashed fabrics, but can be preshrunk if desired. Because of the long fibers, it is a dream to hand or machine quilt, and as easily as the other cottons. You can work in any combination of washed and non-washed batting and fabric, and the quilt retains its integrity. It makes for a very washable quilt; one that is extremely drapeable and soft.

This batting is not a substitute for any of the others discussed in this chapter; it is a batt that fills the needs of quilters in transition from polyester to cotton batting. It is for those who own hundreds of yards of prewashed fabric, but desire a cotton quilt with the texture, comfort, and slight puckering that we so love about old quilts. I have found this batt to be the least intimidating to a quilter just leaving polyester and trying to work through the maze of all the various cottons.

WOOL BATTING

FIG 6.4 *Various wool battings*

Quiltmakers are reviving their interest in wool batting. Many new quilters are asking, "Why wool?" Wool is the fiber of choice when warmth and durability are needed, and we now use it as a substitute for polyester when natural fibers are desirable. The comfort of wool is universally recognized as superior to man-made (plastic) fibers. It is very warm and lofty without being heavy and wiry.

Wool has characteristics that no other fiber provides. First, the wool fiber has built-in crimp, giving it bounce and loft that allows it to always return to its original shape. Wool has a recovery rate from compression of 95%, which is better than any other fiber (polyester averages 73% depending on the type of polyester fiber treatment used). This resiliency provides long-lasting beauty and warmth.

Loft retention is excellent, as the fibers interlock to create airspace, instead of relying solely on resins to glue the airspace together. Wool also has a natural bonding ability that polyester does not have. The fiber is composed of scales overlapping each other. An unbonded batt, if separated by shaking or airing, will reattach to each other in a new position, allowing the fullness to be re-created. Polyester does not have this ability. Airing wool quilts and comforters twice a year restores loft and fullness to the fiber.

Wool batting provides superb insulation. The interlocking fibers breathe, allowing excess heat to disperse away from the body. This allows our skin to remain warm, yet dry. It moderates temperature, so you never get too hot or too cold when sleeping under it. Wool gives warmth without weight. It is naturally hydroscopic and can absorb up to 33% of its own weight in moisture without feeling damp, as opposed to 4% for synthetics and 8% for cottons. This makes it a perfect quilt for a damp, cold climate. Polyester tends to become clammy when damp. Tiny fibers trap air, forming an insulating barrier that gives warmth in a lightweight batt.

Wool batts are naturally mildew resistant and resist moth damage when quilted with cotton fabrics. Moths do not eat cotton, so they cannot get to the wool if its totally covered. Also, moths do not eat the wool fibers unless dirt—their food—is attached to the fibers. The fibers are damaged as the moth eats the dirt. You can protect your quilts, as well as any other wool item, by keeping them clean.

One consideration that is not often thought of is the safety of different fibers. Polyester is used in most quilts made for babies, but if these quilts are ever exposed to fire or high heat, the polyester fibers will melt and the resins on the batt will cause them to flare. This melting process can be extremely dangerous to skin. On the other hand, wool is naturally flame-resistant. When exposed to flames, it smolders at a low temperature and self-extinguishes with a cool ash, making it an extremely safe fiber to use for small children.

Bearding is often considered a problem with wool batts. An unresinated batt is likely to beard when washed, but tests show that it is at its worst after the first wash, and does not get any worse with progressive launderings. By the fourth wash, the bearding should start to disappear, and by the seventh or eighth wash most of the bearded fibers have shed and are not even noticeable. Resinated wool batts tend not to beard at all. Bearding in wool batts is not a permanent problem as it is in polyester.

Be sure to read Chapter 15 before washing a wool quilt. There are specific guidelines you should be aware of before attempting to launder a wool quilt.

Wool batting is made from scoured wool. Thorough scouring removes excess lanolin. The wool is then carded and combed. Combing removes plant and insect particles as well as the shorter, coarser wool fibers. Carding and combing produces unspun wool. To make the batt, it is then opened or "plucked" apart into fluffy fiber. The higher the quality of wool used, the softer and fluffier the batt will be. Quilters have the option of using an "opened" (web) wool batting, a needle-punched wool batting, or a resinated wool batt. The opened batt, used for tied comforters, is fluffier, with loose fiber. Needle-punched wool is made to be quilted. Hobbs Bonded Fibers has produced a new wool batting from loose fibers, which is lightly resinated to resist fiber migration and shifting.

The ability of a wool batting to be washed depends on how the wool is processed. Wool fibers are covered with small scales that interlock and hold the fibers together. If exposed to heat and moisture, the fibers pull together and permanently felt and/or shrink. Modern processing includes shrink-proofing as an essential part of the manufacturing process. It is accomplished in one of two ways:

1 Wet chlorination soaks the wool in a chlorine solution that dissolves the scales on the surface of the wool fiber.

2 Gas chlorination uses chlorine gas, which is filtered through the raw wool to dissolve the scales on the surface of the fiber.

Wet chlorination is the standard method of shrink-proofing wool batting. This process only treats the surface of the wool fiber. The wool fibers will still absorb water during washing, allowing the fibers to swell and any remaining scales to expand. Slight shrinkage may be evident.

COMBED AND OPENED WOOL BATTING

These batts are generally homemade or manufactured by small businesses. Order samples of these batts before purchasing them in any quantity. Some are of beautiful quality, but some are dirty and hardly suitable for quilting.

Encase these combed and opened wool batts in a cheesecloth covering before putting them into quilts. Wool fiber will migrate easily through to the surface of the fabric if not contained.

Cheesecloth comes 44" wide, and I prefer to use 40-gauge weave. Apply it to both sides of the wool batt and baste every 3"-4" using long, loose stitches with a tapestry needle. Finish the edges of the cheesecloth so the batt is totally encased. Now the batting is ready for the layering process. Once this is done, you can quilt or tie every 3"-5" without worry. Quilting distance depends on how you will clean the quilt. Quilt more closely if you plan to wash the quilt, and quilt further apart if you plan to dry-clean.

NEEDLE-PUNCHED WOOL

Taos Mountain Wool Works is a company that produces a superior quality wool batting using the needle-punch process. A uniform quality, Merino-type wool is used. The long, soft wool fiber (intended for worsted fabrics), gives the batt a medium weight and a superior drape.

The fiber is scoured, carded, combed, and plucked into a fluffy fiber web. This web is fed into needle-punching equipment. The needles, which have barbs protruding from the shaft, move through the layer of fibers, and the barbs push the fibers into distorted and tangled arrangements. The web is contained by metal plates above and below so the fibers cannot be pulled or pushed beyond the web layer. As the web moves slowly through the machine, the needles punch as many times as desired for the end product. This process reduces the amount of fiber migration common to wool batts. It also reduces air circulation, making the batt very warm relative to its thickness.

The manufacturer suggests lightly steaming the surfaces of the batt with a steam iron before using. This reduces the risk of migrating fibers. I have done this and still found migrating to be a problem. I suggest that you also encase the batt in cheesecloth. Needle-punched wool batts can be quilted or tied, approximately 3"-5" apart. Quilt closer if cheesecloth is not used.

It is recommended that quilts and comforters with unresinated wool batts be dry-cleaned to prevent shrinkage, but vacuuming, as well as airing on a cloudy, breezy day, is usually sufficient for cleaning. Wool naturally repels dirt. Keep the surface fabrics protected from soiling by putting your wool quilt between a sheet and another blanket. This eliminates any washing problems. If you do decide to wash your quilt, use only tepid wash and rinse water. Use a neutral detergent, such as Orvus Paste®. Handle as you would your very finest cashmere sweater.

HOBBS HEIRLOOM® PREMIUM WOOL

I have worked with Hobbs to produce this premium wool batt for today's quilters. The criteria was to produce a washable, dryable, lightweight, soft, and fluffy batting to substitute for polyester.

This batting is made from $1\frac{1}{2}$"-long fibers. The fibers are chlorine-treated, which is intended to prevent shrinkage. The web that results from these fibers is lightly resinated to provide stability and retard fiber migration.

Heirloom Premium Wool can be quilted up to 3" apart. It is made to be easily washed and dried. It is a similar weight and loft as today's polyester batts, giving a similar look as polyester, but with superior loft retention and comfort. Of all the current wool battings on the market, this is by far the easiest to quilt and live with. It is a must-try for every quilter who loves natural fibers.

With careful washing and correct care of the quilt, Heirloom Premium Wool will endure years of wear, tear, and constant use, allowing the quilt to become a treasured heirloom.

SYNTHETIC FIBERS

Once polyester batting was introduced on the market, quilting took on a new look. Quilters liked its ease of handling, warmth, strength, and low cost. Beginning quilters found success in their attempts without extensive hand quilting. By the late 1970s, polyester was the predominant batting used by quilters, and new quilters were not given any choices. The idea that the batting should complement the quilt was lost for a number of years. Like natural fibers, synthetics have both desirable and undesirable qualities.

A look at how the batts are manufactured will explain why they behave the way they do and help guide you through the maze of products on the market. The battings available for use in quilt making can vary in web formation, the bonding technique used, and the curing or drying process.

Polyester batts are made using either the oriented web or random web (air-lay) process. Oriented webs are made on conventional carding equipment. The fibers are metered and uniformly distributed on a moving belt. Several webs may be superimposed to obtain the desired thickness. The fibers can all be parallel to each other (lengthwise) or placed at right angles to one another by building layers of fibers. When all layers are lengthwise, the web is strong lengthwise, but weak crosswise. With the right-angle fiber layers, strength is found in both directions. The fibers are bonded together either through an adhesive applied to the surface (glazing) or by the addition of heat-sensitive fibers that help seal the final fabric as they soften and fuse with other fibers when heated. This process is characteristic of Mountain Mist Glazene® process polyester batting, both regular weight and Quilt-Light®.

Random webs are made on special machines that suspend the fibers in a rapidly moving air stream. They are then blown or forced onto a continuously moving belt where the web is formed. The fiber arrangement is random, and the web has relatively uniform characteristics. This process is common for what we call "bonded batting" and is characteristic of many brands, including Fairfield Processing's Extra Loft®, Low Loft®, Hi Loft®, and Hobbs Bonded Fibers Poly-Down® battings.

The bonding is achieved either through the application of an adhesive binder, the softening of some fibers in the fiber mix by heat, or the use of solvents that chemically soften some of the fibers so that they will bind the fiber mat together. The mat is stable after the solvent has been removed.

The final stage for both processes is drying and curing. Drying devices include hot-air ovens, heated cans, infrared lights and high-frequency electrical equipment. The choice depends on the particular binding agent.

When examining the characteristics of either of these methods, carefully consider the end use of the quilt, as well as the quilting distance to be used. Choose only premium, packaged batts that are intended for quilts. Many polyester batts are too stiff and thick for quilts, and are intended for craft purposes, upholstery, and commercial uses.

Mountain Mist produces an oriented web batt of 100% polyester fiber that is finished with a Glazene finish. This process gives a quilt different characteristics than does a bonded batt. Because the bonding is achieved by applying the resin to only the surface of the web, the inside fibers are loose and free. This can create some drawbacks where bearding is concerned; however, the more quilting that is put into the batting, the less it tends to beard. Very close, dense stitching can be done without the characteristic stiffness that most polyester batts show. It also allows you to quilt very closely in one area and further apart in another without distortion.

Suggested distance for spacing quilting stitches is from $1/4$" to a maximum of 2"–$2^1/2$" apart. The more space between stitch lines, the more shifting and bearding is likely.

Mountain Mist polyester batts have the appearance and loft of cotton. This allows the quiltmaker to have the somewhat antique look of cotton without its disadvantages: shrinkage, weight, and the need for extremely close quilting. It is also very easy to work with on the machine. It is not springy and it does not drag under the needle as the thicker polyesters do.

We have been told over the last decade that bonded batting was the only safe batting to use, but no explanation of "safe" was ever given. Thus, it was put into every quilt made, with little or no consideration of its weak points. We were also told that it could be quilted 6"–8" apart, which we are now seeing is a major error. Quilts made in the past 15 years with polyester batting are aging poorly.

The bonding process was invented to add loft artificially to the batt, but there is no more actual fiber in a one-pound thick batt than there is in a one-pound flatter batt. Therefore, over time, the bonded batts will lose their loft. Further, a process of stretching and roping occurs as the resins and air space break down. Roping is evidenced by the migration and attraction of the synthetic fibers joining together and creating a firm mass of fiber. This "rope" then twists slightly, leaving small ridges in the batting. Purchased comforters do this after several washings. It can be caused by poor quality product, under-quilting, or both. On the other hand, bonded battings offer warmth with little weight, the ability to be quilted up to 4" apart, and the puffy look that enhances so many quilts.

Often quilters shop for batting by weight, such as a 3- or 4-ounce batting. Most of the weight of a batt comes from its bonding additives. Because every company uses a different bonding agent in varying amounts to bond the fibers together, it is not possible to compare products by weight. The weight can also be affected by the fiber content and the thickness of the fiber used when layering, making the thickness of the batt the prime consideration, not the weight.

Needle-punched polyester batting is also available for use in quilting. Because it tends to be denser and stiffer than the other polyesters, it is desirable for quilted projects, such as wallhangings, placemats, garments, pillows, etc., but not for quilts.

There are different ways to produce needle-punched batting. The batt is laid with five or more layers across the width of the belt. One method runs the batt through a machine with rows of needles that pound and compress the product to a uniform thickness. It comes out with approximately 10% of the original loft. Another method uses barbed needles that curl and intertwine the fibers into a dense batt. The third method sends the batt of thermoplastic fibers through a machine using hot needles. The needles melt the parts of the fibers that they touch, causing them to fuse together to form a more stable batt. Some brands of needle-punched batting are Traditional™ from Fairfield Processing Corporation, Pellon® Fleece, and Thermore® from Hobbs. These batts are more likely to beard at first because the fibers on top are not interlocked. Washing should eventually wear the loose fibers off, making the batt more stable.

The bearding syndrome of polyester battings must be taken seriously because once it starts, there is no cure. The process often does not begin until the resin breaks down from usage, and it can last up to three years. Choose good quality, high thread-count fabrics. If lower-quality fabrics or blends are used, expect bearding to be a problem. To camouflage bearding on dark fabrics, Hobbs Bonded Fibers has produced a charcoal gray batting, Poly-Down-DK®.

One of the ways manufacturers are trying to improve synthetic battings is by using "slick," hollow-core fibers. The theory is that the slick fibers will not stick together as badly as regular fibers, cutting down on the compression rate, or loss of loft. They are also supposed to reduce static and bearding. Because they use softer fibers, they provide more warmth. Hobbs Bonded Fibers has produced a batting called Poly-Down 100% Loftguard® Polyester that is made of these slick fibers.

THERMORE® BY HOBBS BONDED FIBERS

Consumers need to be aware that all synthetic battings are made of thermoplastic fibers, which are very heat-sensitive. This could pose a threat if the finished product is to be exposed to direct heat. The fiber will melt instantly, and the melting spreads rapidly. Also, resins and bonding agents are potentially combustible chemicals. These factors need to be considered if the end product is to be used by small children, people who smoke, or for sleeping arrangements near hot registers or fireplaces. Also consider that synthetics do not breathe. For some, a polyester quilt is like covering up with a sheet of plastic, causing the skin to perspire and body heat to build up. For others, the added warmth is needed.

In short, buyer beware. Manufacturers are researching and developing new products that will eliminate as many of the hazards as possible. However, we as consumers need to use personal judgment. Test all materials to be sure that they will perform the way you expect.

THE BATTING TEST

I would imagine that by now you are completely confused by all the choices available to you. Remember, confusion is the beginning of knowledge. I suggest that you obtain samples of, and thoroughly test, every batting available and every new batting product that appears on the market. If you will take the time to do the tests, you will know everything you need to make your quilts have the exact look you want, and know how they will age, how close you need to quilt them, etc. You truly have no valid excuse not to do these tests. The information you glean from them is invaluable.

First, collect three 14" squares of every batting you can find. If you have trouble obtaining some of the battings listed below, please contact me at the address on page 176 and I can make the samples available to you. You will need only three squares if the batting cannot be preshrunk. If it can be preshrunk, you will need an additional two squares (preshrunk) for a total of five. Make sure that the brands are labeled so you know which battings you are working with.

Next, create a pile of 14" squares of preshrunk muslin (quilt-shop quality ONLY) and a pile of non washed muslin squares. Label the squares with a permanent marker to identify those washed and non-washed. In the center of each of these squares, draw a perfect 6" square with permanent marker.

For the backing squares, sew a 7¹/₄" strip of black cotton to a 7¹/₄" strip of muslin. Cut these strips into 14" squares. You will need a pile of these made from preshrunk and non-washed fabric.

You are now ready to layer the batting and fabric together. Do so in the following order:

1 one piece of non-washed batting with non-washed fabric—top and back.

2 one piece of non-washed batting with prewashed fabric—top and back.

3 one piece of prewashed batting with non-washed fabric—top and back.

4 one piece of prewashed batting with prewashed fabric—top and back.

Label the muslin square with the brand of batting, whether the batt is prewashed or not, and whether the fabric is prewashed or not.

You should have one square of non-washed batting left. Copy the Sample Sheet on page 64 and staple the remaining batting square to it. Use it as a control sample for future comparison against new batts of the same brand to compare for consistency. If you find that the batting looks and feels different from the one you tested, you may want to run new tests on the new batt to see if it will perform differently than the original.

Now you will need to quilt the samples. If you are a hand quilter as well as a machine quilter, hand quilt half of the block, and machine quilt the other half. On the form, make a note of whether you enjoyed quilting this batt, and which method you preferred. If you are not a hand quilter, simply machine quilt the entire block. Quilt the distances that are within the guidelines given throughout this chapter, or refer to the chart on page 62 for quick reference.

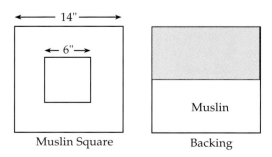

FIG. 6.5 *Fabric squares for batting test*

This is an excellent time to experiment with various threads and needles. The rayon, metallic, and cotton embroidery threads will react differently to different battings. Work out the tensions and problems here, instead of on your quilt. Also experiment with the various needles listed in the equipment chapter with these different threads. Use these batting samples to learn as much as possible. Also note any tension adjustments that were needed for that particular batting, or differences in tension settings for various types and brands of threads and needles. Stitch-length settings can also be noted for each batt.

Once quilted, measure the 6" square. Using the measurements in the following formula, compute to see if you have lost any size from quilting (known as contraction). Many battings will cause a size loss in the finished size of the quilt simply from the take-up that occurs in the quilting process.

$$\% \text{ of shrinkage} = \frac{\textit{Original} - \textit{Final}}{\textit{Original measurement}} \times 100$$

Make a note of any size changes.

Once you have done this, now is the time to wash and dry the quilt blocks. Wash and dry how you would care for your finished quilts. Recommended care instructions can be found in Chapter 15.

Once you have dried the blocks, organize them so that all samples from the same brand of batting are together. Look at them and start to form your own opinions. Is one sample too wrinkled and another too flat? Do you really like the sample with the unwashed fabric and unwashed batting, but the sample with the prewashed fabric and non-washed batting did not work out too well? Start to eliminate the combinations that distort the blocks or just don't appeal to you. Be aware of your feelings toward the look of the sample. You will find that you may like one combination, but your best friend prefers another. This is OK. Quilting is a very personal skill, and we should be making quilts that appeal to us, and look like what we like, not just trying to please everyone else. If you like the finished result—go for it. It's your quilt.

Next, re-measure the 6" square in the center of the block, and rework the shrinkage formula. This gives you the total amount of size loss due to contraction and shrinkage from washing and drying. Now you can use these findings to determine if you need to make your quilt top a bit larger than the finished quilt needs to be, based on how the batting performs. Shrinkage doesn't need to be feared; learn about it instead and make it work for you.

The reason for the black on the back is to help look for bearding problems. Are tiny fibers migrating to the surface of the fabric? Are lots of fibers migrating? If so, this batt would not be appropriate for dark fabrics. Also look at the top of the block. Is the dark color shadowing through the batting to the top of the block and discoloring the top surface? This is a typical problem with polyester battings. The batting is transparent, allowing the color of the backing to shadow through to the top. It also dilutes the color of lights, making them appear slightly gray or tired. Cotton battings are opaque, and light cannot pass through them. You will not see the color coming from the back to the top on a cotton batt because of this. The cotton also keeps the true color in the top fabric by providing a "backing" that light cannot penetrate to dilute. If you want to put a dark backing on a light quilt top, you can if you are wise in your batting choice.

Once you have filled out the form, wash and dry all the samples again. Continue to do this week after week. Make a mark on each square every time they are washed and dried. Examine the samples after five washings, again after 10, and so forth. After 10 or 15 washings, see how the batting is holding up. Is this a batting you could use in a baby quilt and wash weekly, if not daily, and have it hold up? Or is it fragile and not aging well under such use? Determine where and when these battings would be appropriate in the quilts you make. Not all quilts lay on closet shelves, but not all quilts are on kids' beds either.

Things you should ask yourself when choosing a batt for a particular quilt:

❖ Do I want natural, synthetic, or a blended fiber batt?

❖ Do I want it thin or thick?

❖ Do I want it flat or fluffy?

❖ Do I want to hand quilt it or machine quilt it?

❖ How close do I want to quilt this quilt?

❖ Do I need this quilt for warmth, or do I want a cooler quilt—is it for summer, spring, fall, or winter temperatures?

❖ Is the quilt going to be washed a lot or just for show?

❖ Is the quilt going to hang on the wall, or lay on a bed?

❖ Do I need the quilt to look antique, or contemporary—should it be smooth or pucker?

If you can answer all these questions for every quilt you make, you will be matching the appropriate batting to every quilt top. This information is not available in a book or classroom. The only way to truly learn about batting is to do the samples. But I know that most of you won't bother to do this. You will probably say that you don't have time to waste on muslin samples. But do you have the time or money to invest in a quilt top that you love, only to be disappointed in the final result because the batting does not look right?

Think about it this way—as you get further into this book, and start practicing the machine-quilting techniques, you will need samples to practice on. What if you were to spend some time and collect the ingredients and layer them together as suggested above. Then when you sit down to practice your quilting skills, you already have the materials ready. But instead of throwing away your practice blocks, you set them aside to test. As you practice, you are not wasting an hour of time, an ounce of batting, or a yard of fabric. You are not only learning to quilt, you are developing an invaluable reference library of brands and types of battings, as well as what combinations they can be successfully used in and how well they wear with repeated launderings. What else could you ask from just a few hours of preparation and practice?

SUGGESTIONS FOR WORKING WITH BATTINGS

SPLICING BATTING

Battings come in various sizes, but often you need a larger size than a particular type is available in. You will need to splice two batts together to get the needed size. Traditionally, two even straight edges are butted and whip stitched together. The problem with this method is that the splice becomes evident, appearing as a "break line" through the quilt, as well as a ridge from the whipstitching. Instead of butting two straight edges together, overlap the two pieces of batting 6"-8". Cut a serpentine line through both layers. The gradual undulating curves will butt together perfectly once the end of each layer is removed.

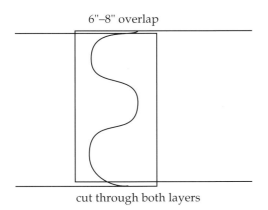

6"–8" overlap

cut through both layers

FIG. 6.6 Splicing batting

Hand stitch, using about ¹/₂" long, loose herringbone stitches. This serpentine stitch will eliminate any unsightly evidence as to where you made the splice.

FIG. 6.7 Herringbone stitch illustration for joining batting

BATTING GRAINLINE

Most battings have a definite grainline. The exceptions are the needle-punched battings that are so stable that one direction is no different than the other. To find the grainline of the batt, gently pull on it from both directions. Like fabric, the length of the batt is stronger and less able to stretch than the cross grain. This grain should be considered when layering a quilt, as it will determine which direction you will quilt first.

Referring to Chapter 8 about linings for whole quilts, look at the illustrations showing the grain of the lining going across the width of the quilt. This saves fabric, but if the strong grain of the batting is going the opposite direction of the strong grain of the lining, it may cause distortion and difficulty during the quilting process. Consider running the grain of the batting and lining in the same direction. When you begin to quilt, you will quilt the lengthwise (strong) grain seams first—in this case across the width of the quilt—instead of the seams going the length of the quilt. This keeps the machine from stretching the grain and causing unnecessary distortion.

Another consideration is how a quilt hangs on the wall. Always make sure that the lengthwise grains of both the batting and lining is going the length of the quilt as it hangs on the wall. Gravity can pull and stretch the fabric, and especially the batting, until it sags and distorts terribly. If the stretchy grainline is being pulled constantly by gravity, you can imagine the damage and appearance. On the other hand, the lack of stretch in the lengthwise grain will slow this problem considerably. This will be discussed again in Chapter 11.

Brand Name	Fiber Content	Quilting Distance	Appearance
Mountain Mist 100% Natural Cotton	100% cotton	$1/4$"- 1"	Antique appearance. Puckers from shrinkage.
Mountain Mist Blue Ribbon	100% cotton	$1/4$"- 2"	Flat, thin, antique appearance.
Mountain Mist Cotton Choice	100% cotton with polyester scrim	6"- 8"	Flat, thin.
Morning Glory Old Fashioned	100% cotton with polyester scrim	4"- 6"	Has leaf and stem particles left in for old look. Puckers slightly from shrinkage. Older looking quilts.
Morning Glory Clearly Bleached	100% cotton	1"- 6"	Flat, thin.
Morning Glory Clearly Unbleached	100% cotton	1"- 6"	Flat, thin.
P & B or First Run Fabrics Double Brushed Cotton Flannelette	100% cotton High quality with adequate thread count.	Variable	Flat, very thin.
Fairfield Cotton Classic	80% cotton 20% polyester	$1/4$"- 3"	Flat, thin.
Hobbs Bonded Fibers Heirloom Premium Cotton	80% cotton 20% polyester	$1/4$" - 3"	Slight loft, low shrinkage.
Hobbs Bonded Fibers Heirloom Premium Wool	100% wool	1" - 3"	Resilient, low loft, soft, drapable.
Warm & Natural Warm Products Inc.	100% cotton with polyester scrim	up to 10"	Flat, thin.
Generic Wool (from numerous sources)	100% wool	1" - 4"	Puffy, resilient.
Mountain Mist Glazene Process 100% Polyester and Mountain Mist Quilt-Light	100% polyester	$1/8$"- $2^1/2$"	Thin to moderately puffy.
Fairfield Low Loft, Extra Loft, High Loft	100% polyester	2"- 4"	Moderate to high lift. Various lofts range from $1/4$" - 3" thick.
Hobbs Bonded Fibers Thermore	100% polyester	3"- 4"	Very thin.

Characteristics	Uses	Sizes Available (in inches)
5%+ shrinkage. Not bonded. Layers stick together. Cool in summer; warm in winter. Adjusts to body temperature. Drapeable, cuddly. Breathes. Cannot be preshrunk.	Antique quilt tops, antique quilt reproductions, wall quilts, baby quilts, hot pads.	81 x 96 , 81 x 108
Moderate to no shrinkage. Bonded. Layers stick together. Breathes. Cool in summer. Adjusts to body temperature. Cannot be preshrunk.	Antique quilt tops, antique quilt reproductions, wall quilts, baby quilts, hot pads, clothing.	45 x 60, 90 x 108
Can be stiff if quilted too heavily, needle-punched felt type batting. Can be presoaked if desired.	Wall quilts, garments, craft projects, Home-dec projects.	By yard, 34 x 72 By yard, 90 wide
Can be preshrunk or not. Flatter appearance. Heavier weight quilts. Needle-punched for fiber stability. Can be stiff if overquilted.	Wallhangings, throws, bedspreads, craft projects, quilts.	45 x 60, 90 x 108 120 x 120 By yard, 90 wide
Bleached fiber in a needle-punched batt. Soft, drapeable, stable.	Quilts, wallhangings, miniatures, garments.	36 x 90, 45 x 60 90 x 108 By yard, 90 wide
Needle-punched, Soft, drapeable, stable.	Quilts, wallhangings, miniatures, garments.	36 x 90, 45 x 60 90 x 108 By yard, 90 wide
Can shrink to give antique appearance. No loft. Lightweight.	Baby quilts, lap robes, summer-weight coverlets, miniature quilts, tablecloths, placemats, clothing.	By yard, 45 wide
Moderate to no shrinkage. Shrinkage allowance should be checked (refer to page 59). Can be presoaked if desired. Breathes. Cool in summer. Can be split for miniatures.	Quilts, wall quilts, baby quilts, tablecloths, placemats, clothing, miniatures.	36 x 45, 81 x 96
Extremely easy cotton to hand quilt. Will shrink slightly. Durable, drapeable, soft, warm.	Quilts, baby quilts, wallhangings, garments.	90 x 108, 120 x 120 By yard, 96 wide
Very warm in cold, damp climates. More comfortable than polyester. Very little or no bearding. Resinated.	Quilts, garments, lap quilts, throws.	90 x 108
Can be stiff if over quilted. Should be prewashed to remove oil from seeds.	Wall quilts, crafts, garments.	34 x 45, 90 x 108, 120 x 120 By yard, 90 wide.
Must be encased in cheesecloth. High resilience. Warm in cold, damp climates.	Tied comforters and quilts.	Varies
Fibers shift to fill space available. Can be quilted extremely close without getting stiff. Does not shrink. Look and feel of cotton. Heat sensitive.	Bed quilts, lap quilts.	45 x 60, 72 x 90 81 x 96, 90 x 108 120 x 120
Warm, lightweight, heat sensitive. Stretches and distorts if hung. Low recovery from compression. Does not shrink.	Bed quilts, lap quilts, pillows, stuffing.	45 x 60, 72 x 90 81 x 96, 90 x 108 120 x 120
Extremely drapeable. Easy to quilt. Lightweight. Does not beard.	Garments, miniature quilts, wallhangings, quilts.	45 x 54, 90 x 108 By yard, 90 wide.

BATTING SAMPLE TEST SHEET

Brand name: _____

Fiber content: _____

Sizes available: _____

Recommended quilting distance: _____

How did it needle?

    Hand: _____

    Machine: _____

Thread used:

    Top: _____

    Bobbin: _____

Needle used: _____

Appearance after quilting? _____

Bearding? _____

Shadowing through? _____

Contraction when quilted? _____

Shrinkage after washing? _____

Opinion of appearance after washing:

Which combination did I like best? _____

Appearance after 5 washings: _____

        after 10 washings: _____

        after 15 washings: _____

Quilts I have used this batting in: _____

Other comments: _____

_____

_____

_____

_____

_____

_____

_____

_____

WEDDING GOWN

Machine quilted by Harriet Hargrave using free-motion, stipple, and echo quilting techniques; DMC 50/2 cotton embroidery thread; Fairfield Cotton Classic® batting

AUNT LIBBY'S ATTIC

Machine pieced and machine quilted by Sandy Espenshield, Atlanta, GA using hanging diamond grid quilting; nylon thread; Mountain Mist® 100% natural cotton batting
39" x 49"

ANTIQUE QUILTED PETTICOAT & BIB

Early 1900's quilted garments totally made by machine; cotton thread; three layers of fabric (no batting); collection of Harriet Hargrave

A WINTER SLEIGH RIDE

Original pattern by Jean Johnson; hand appliquéd and machine quilted by Sue Rasmussen,
Simi Valley, CA using free-motion, stipple, and grid quilting techniques; nylon thread;
Mountain Mist® 100% polyester batting
39" x 49"

REMEMBER ME

Pieced and machine quilted by Mary Pilger Lambert, Eureka, IL
using straight line, ditch, and free-motion quilting techniques; nylon thread;
Hobbs Heirloom® premium cotton batting
55" x 71"

BARGELLO

Pieced and quilted by Mary Pilger Lambert, Eureka, IL using free-motion line quilting; nylon thread; Hobbs Heirloom® premium cotton batting
44" x 60"

SUMMER LEAVES

Machine quilted by Jean Lohmar, Galesburg, IL using free-motion quilting; nylon thread
25" x 25"

TULIPS BY
THE PATH

*Machine appliquéd and quilted by Harriet
Hargrave using echo, stipple, and random
quilting techniques; nylon thread;
Hobbs Heirloom® premium cotton batting
42" x 42"*

BLUE MEDALLION

Machine pieced and quilted by Harriet Hargrave using ditch, free-motion, continuous curve, and echo quilting techniques; nylon thread; Mountain Mist® 100% polyester batting 68" x 84"

SMELL THE SPRING FLOWERS

*Machine pieced and quilted by Betty Gilliam,
Stillwater, OK using continuous curve,
stipple, and free-motion quilting techniques;
Mountain Mist® Quilt Lite polyester batting
54" x 54"*

❖ PART THREE ❖
TECHNIQUES

HEIRLOOM
MACHINE
QUILTING

74

QUILT-AS-YOU-GO TECHNIQUES

As you begin to discover the excitement and fun of machine quilting, you will want to start with small projects and work up to larger ones. Depending on the chosen batting and the size of the quilt, you may prefer to quilt in sections as opposed to quilting one large, bulky piece. This gives more maneuverability than when working with a large quilt that is all in one piece. This chapter will teach you how to quilt-as-you-go so that you can choose the method best for you.

Before assembling the quilt blocks to make your quilt top, make a graph of the quilt top on paper to determine section divisions. Use the following to figure the available width of the lining fabrics when planning your quilt:

❖ Lining fabric is likely to be 45" wide. Once you subtract 1" for selvages and 1" for seam allowances, approximately 42" of usable width remains to accommodate the quilt sections. Base your section sizes on a 42"-wide piece of fabric.

Let's work through an example. You are making a quilt, with no borders, which measures 80" by 90" finished. You are using a 10" block. The blocks are set together eight blocks wide and nine blocks long. The 80" can be divided evenly by two to obtain two 40" sections across the width of the quilt. The lining (42") will accommodate this. The 90" length can be divided into three sections, each 30" long. This will give you a section that is easy to handle.

The quilt top shown in Figure 7.1 is 80" by 90". The top is divided evenly into six sections, each four blocks wide by three blocks long. Each unit measures 40" by 30" keeping within the lining width.

Before setting the blocks together, lay them out in order on the floor to make sure the pattern repeat is correct. Then sew them together into the section sizes determined. It may be necessary for you to label or number the sections to keep them in their proper order as you work.

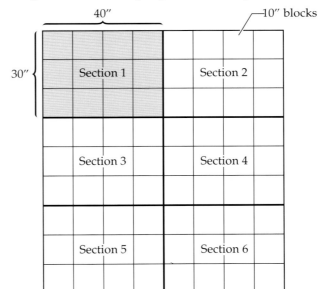

FIG. 7.1 Dividing quilt into sections

Once the sections are constructed, determine the size needed for the batting and lining. These need to be at least 2" larger than each quilt section on all four sides to allow for contraction while quilting, as well as extra ease when joining the seams.

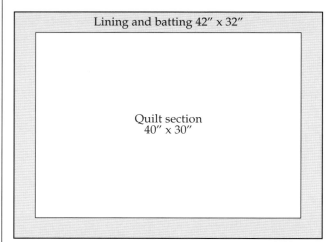

FIG. 7.2 *Layered quilt section*

Lining and batting for this example would need to be cut 42" by 32" (Figure 7.2).

Your quilt top will not always divide into an even number of blocks in each section. Figure 7.3 shows a quilt top that finishes 77" by 84". If the blocks are 7" square, they are placed 11 across the width of the quilt and 12 down the length. When you draw a graph on paper of your quilt, put six blocks across in one section and five blocks across the other section. The length can be divided evenly into three sections. This gives you three sections that are six blocks across and four blocks long (42" by 28") and three sections that are five blocks across and four blocks long (35" by 28"). Now figure the size of the batting and lining by adding 2" for contraction and joining seams.

This example demonstrates possible problems with lining sizes. You can see that one section is 42" wide. When placed with a 42" piece of lining, there is no allowance for contraction. You need to run the lengthwise grain of the fabric across the width of the quilt. The lining width of 42" will easily accommodate the 28" length of each section. An alternative to this is to divide the quilt into more sections, accommodating the lining by keeping the width of each section less than 40" wide.

Or, the top section can be constructed so that you have long strips the full length of the quilt. This requires less finishing on the back since there are fewer pieces. Depending on your level of comfort with machine quilting, this option should be considered.

An alternate method of dividing the quilt into sections, if the design allows, is to split the center block itself (Figure 7.4). Even patch designs (two-, four-, six-patch blocks, etc.) are excellent for this method. A 77" by 84" quilt, containing even patch blocks, is easily split into six equal-sized sections. Figure 7.4 shows each section containing five full blocks, and half of the center block.This division also allows the lining seam to be centered on the back of the quilt.

Note: If you are adding borders to your quilt, they must be considered when drawing diagrams for figuring lining and batting sizes.

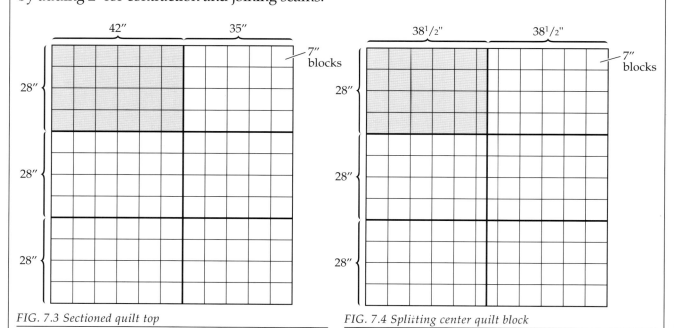

FIG. 7.3 *Sectioned quilt top*

FIG. 7.4 *Splitting center quilt block*

Add their width to the quilt sections when figuring section size. Borders are added after the quilt sections are quilted and joined, but batting and lining allowances must be made before the quilting process. When all sections are joined, there is a margin of batting and lining left to accommodate the border piece (Figure 7.12).

LAYERING QUILT-AS-YOU-GO SECTIONS

Work smaller units on a tabletop or counter when layering. Use masking or drafting tape to tape the lining down to the surface. Stretch it, keeping it tight and free from sagging and shifting. Place the batting on top of the lining, keeping the edges even. Lining and batting should always be the same size. Be sure to place the quilt top sections onto the batting and lining evenly, leaving slightly less allowance around the edges joined to another section.

After placing the quilt top section on the batting, label each section to identify its position within the quilt. Check that the patchwork pattern meets correctly with the adjoining section. To avoid a section mix-up, lay the sections out on the floor. Double-check that each section is in the proper place before quilting.

Refer to Chapter 9 for layering techniques. If you have layered and pinned the quilt sections properly, the quilting will be trouble-free. Improper or insufficient layering techniques can lead to lumping and puckering of both the back and the front of the quilt.

After the sections are layered, they are ready to be quilted. Read and practice the techniques given in Chapters 11, 12, and 13 to determine what type of quilting is appropriate.

Note: When quilting a quilt-as-you-go section, be sure to begin your stitching on the section edges that will eventually be joined to another section. Begin the stitching at least 1" in from these edges. This allows any excess fullness that might be present to be eased to the outer edges. It also allows for a margin of unstitched area, enabling you to seam the sections together. The quilting lines will be connected later, once the sections are joined.

QUILT-AS-YOU-GO COMES TOGETHER

After quilting the sections, join them into one large piece before adding borders and binding.

Lay the quilt sections out on the floor to check proper position. Join the sections vertically first, creating rows the length of the quilt. You will be sewing horizontal seams. Lay the two sections to be joined on a flat surface with the lining side up. Pin back the lining and batting, exposing the wrong side of the quilt top. With right sides together, stitch the two sections, matching all seams, points, and corners. Sew a $1/4$" seam, or sew the same measurement used in the piecing of the blocks (Figure 7.5).

FIG. 7.5 Blocks sewn together

On the right side of the quilt, lightly press the seam allowance to one side using a warm iron. Press all seams in that row the same direction. Alternate the pressing direction from one row to another. Continue this process until all sections are joined in their respective rows (Figure 7.6).

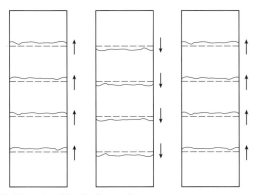

FIG. 7.6 Joining blocks for each row

Lay all the sections on a flat surface with the lining side up. Remove the batting and lining pins. Smooth the batting, laying one side on top of the other. Cut through the two layers of batting so that the two pieces butt together (Figure 7.7). Using a herringbone stitch (Figures 7.8 and 7.9), connect the batting edges together to prevent shifting. Repeat for all seams in each row.

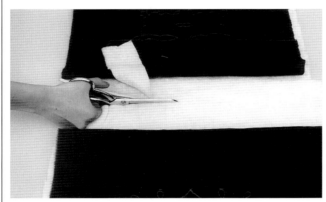

FIG 7.7 Trimming the batting

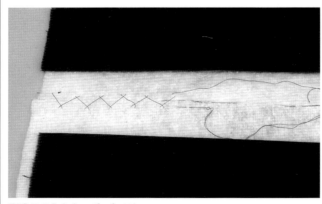

FIG 7.8 Joining the batting

FIG. 7.9 Herringbone stitch illustration

When the batting is secured, finish the lining seams by using the following method: Turn the sections over so that the quilt top faces up. Place pins every $1^1/_2$" along the seam that joins the sections. The pins should be pushed to the back so their points stand upright when the sections are turned over. Now turn the sections over again so the lining faces up. Fold the lining back on each side so the fold rests against the pin markers. Pin each folded edge in place. Remove the pin markers. Press the folded edges, then remove the remaining pins. Repeat this method for each section (Figure 7.10).

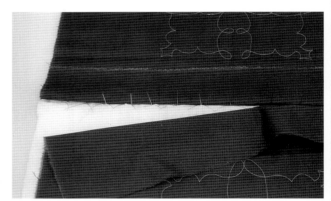

FIG. 7.10 Pin marking for lining seam placement

Unfold the pressed lining edge. Trim excess lining to within $1/_2$" from the crease (Figure 7.10). Lay the lining of Section 1 out flat. Smooth any ripples between the quilting and the edge. Fold the lining edge of Section 2 under along the creased line (Figure 7.11). Match the fold of Section 2 to the creased line of Section 1. Beginning in the center of the line, pin baste every inch through all layers, stopping 2" from the end of the lining. Lift the 2" section of the lining away from the batting and pin. This area needs to be left free to accommodate joining one row to another. Blindstitch with $1/_8$" stitches, using a single thread the same color as the lining.

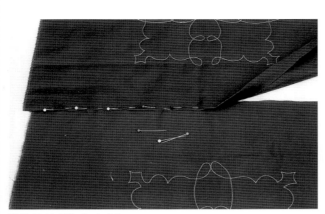

FIG. 7.11 *Blindstitching seam*

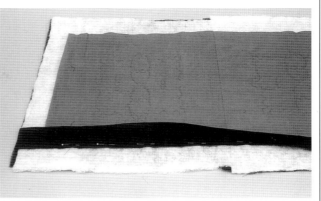

FIG. 7.12 *Attaching border*

Note: Be sure the 2" on the ends are kept free of the batting while blindstitching. Also make sure that your blindstitches do not show through to the quilt top. Repeat this for the remaining seams in each row. The folded lining closures should all be lapped in the same direction.

On the quilt top, connect any quilting lines over the seams just made by connecting the sections. Now you are ready to join the rows. Stitch Row 1 to Row 2, matching all seams, points, and corners. Press the seam to one side. Repeat the same techniques for trimming the batting and folding the lining as you did to join the sections.

After the long seams are finished, add the borders. Measure the length of the quilt through the center of the quilt. Measure the border fabric to be the same length and sew the lengthwise borders onto each side. The border can be sewn through all three layers (top, batting, and lining) or added to the quilt top section only. When the border is opened and smoothed over the batting, there is sufficient batting and lining to accommodate it (Figure 7.12).

Quilt-as-you-go is only one method to prepare your quilt top for machine quilting. It does offer the beginner more maneuverability and ease of bulk than doing the whole quilt at once. This method also allows you to work with thick, bulky battings in large quilts. As your skills increase, you will find it preferable to do many of your quilts as whole quilts. The whole-quilt methods are explained in Chapters 8, 9, and 10.

LINING AND BATTING FOR WHOLE QUILTS

achine quilting a large top requires special handling, but it can be done more easily by following the methods presented in this unit. As with quilt-as-you-go, the whole-quilt method eliminates the need to join sections together and add borders after the quilting is completed.

Lining should be of the same fiber content as the top of the quilt. If you have used polyester blends in the piecing, the lining should also be a blend. If your top is 100% cotton, use only 100% cotton for the back or lining. If you have prewashed your fabrics before piecing your top, be sure to prewash your lining. Allow for 3% shrinkage in lining when figuring yardage. If you have not prewashed your fabric, do not prewash your lining.

Consider whether to use prints or solids. Muslin and bleached cotton, as well as solid colors, are traditional lining fabrics that really show off your quilting. If you are new to machine quilting, you may want to use a print. Small mistakes and uneven stitches are not as conspicuous on a print as they are on solids.

If you have light solids in the quilt top, dark linings can change the appearance of the top fabric, especially when using polyester battings. An example is using white in the quilt top, and a navy blue lining. If you use a polyester batt, the blue lining will cause the white fabric in the top to appear gray. Use cotton batting to eliminate this effect. Refer to the batting samples you have made from Chapter 6 to see which battings will allow you to use dark backings on light quilt tops.

FIGURING YARDAGE FOR LINING AND BATTINGS

When figuring yardage for the lining, allow for contraction. This is the width and length of the fabric used by the loft (thickness) of the batting, as well as by the stitching during the quilting process.

If you use a polyester batting $1/2$" thick or more, you will need to allow 3"–4" extra batting and lining per side than the size of the quilt top. Cotton, cotton blend, and thin polyester battings need to be $1^1/2$"–2" larger on all sides than the quilt top. This excess is needed when machine quilting because the feed dogs tend to take in the lining fabric, and the presser foot flattens out the top, making the top layer larger. The thickness of the batting determines how much fabric is used in the loft, or puff, between the quilting lines. The thicker the batting, the more fabric required to accommodate the loft. A common complaint of machine quilting is that by the time you get to the edge of the quilt, you have 2" more quilt top than lining. This method of figuring yardage helps eliminate this problem.

Generally, 45"-wide yard goods are used for lining. Sheeting in 90" and 108" widths is also available in white and natural and more recently, in limited colors. Bed sheets are also used. These wider fabrics eliminate the need for seams in the lining. Be mindful of thread count and fiber content when shopping for sheets and wide sheeting fabrics for your linings. Sheets are not really recommened for use as quilt backs. The thread count of percale is much too high to hand or machine quilt. Stay with muslin weave sheets. The thread count is lower, but generally the fiber content of these sheets is a blend of cotton and polyester. I recommend you stay away from using sheets unless absolutely necessary.

Seaming is necessary when using 45"-wide fabric. Remember, it has a usable finished width of 40"–42". You cannot back an 87"-wide quilt top with just two widths of 45" fabric. You will have to subtract at least 1" for selvages and another 1" for seam allowances per width.

Sketch your quilt on paper to keep your figures accurate. Always allow for contraction. If you machine quilt an item and cut the lining and batting the same size as the quilt and then quilt it, the top piece will always push off the edge before you are finished. This shift is caused by the pressure of the presser foot pushing the top fabric, and by not allowing for the amount of fabric it takes to "puff up" between the quilting lines. By allowing 2"–4" extra backing and batting on all sides of the quilt top, you will eliminate the problems of fabric shortage and shifting.

To make the lining wide enough, at least one seam will be needed. Usually the seams run vertically with the quilt, but they may run either vertically or horizontally, whichever makes the most efficient use of the fabric. If more than one seam is required, try to balance the location of the panels so that the lining sections are balanced. Join the lengths together using a $^1/_2$" seam. Cut away the selvages and sew $^1/_2$" from the edge, or sew $^3/_4$" with the selvages left on. Clip through the selvage every 1" to prevent puckering along the seam. Press the seam allowances open.

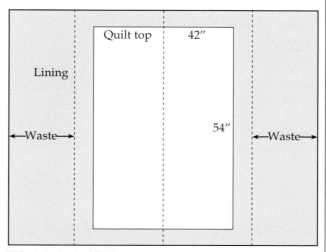

FIG. 8.1 Vertical lining seam

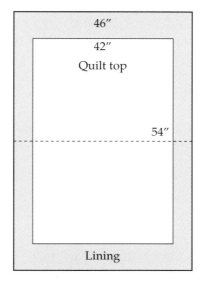

FIG. 8.2 Horizontal lining seam

SMALL QUILTS

Let's work through some examples.
Note: All examples assume you are using
$^1/_4$"-thick batting, which requires 2" allowance
on all sides for contraction.

The most economical way to finish a small
quilt is to keep it under 42". However, if the
quilt is wider than 42", the lining needs to be
seamed. Use simple math to see how to use
the fabric efficiently.

Vertical seam method: The quilt is 42" by 54".
After adding for contraction, the lining should
measure 46" by 58", allowing for 2" on all
sides. This requires two lengths of fabric,
each 58". This is a total of $3^1/_4$ yards. Notice
the waste from the excess width (Figure 8.1).

Horizontal seam method: If we run the seam
horizontally, we need two lengths of lining
46", or $2^2/_3$ yards. This is a more efficient use
of the width of the fabric, as well as requiring
less yardage (Figure 8.2).

TWIN- AND DOUBLE-SIZED QUILTS

Standard-size twin and double-bed quilts
need two lengths of lining fabric to accommodate their width. Some queen-size quilts can
also follow these guides. Be sure to check
your measurements.

If the quilt is 74" by 85", you need two
lengths of 45"-wide lining fabric. Adding 4"
for contraction, you get 89". Divide 89" by 36"
(1 yard), which is $2^1/_2$ yards each (Figure 8.3).
You will need 2 lengths, $2^1/_2$ yards each, for a
total of 5 yards. Add 3% for shrinkage if you
plan to prewash the fabric.

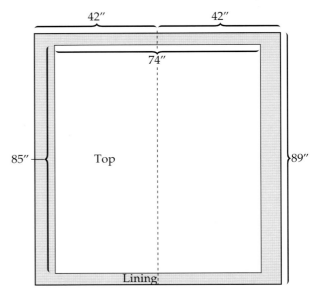

FIG. 8.3 *Utilizing lining with vertical seam*

Let's practice figuring for horizontal seams
(Figure 8.4). It takes three widths to cover
the 89" of length for the quilt. There's a lot
of waste from the width of the lining:
3 by 42" = 126" when we only need 89".
Each length would be $2^1/_6$ yards long
(78" by 36" = $2^1/_6$ yards) times the 3 lengths
needed. This equals $6^1/_2$ yards. This would
not be an efficient use of fabric.

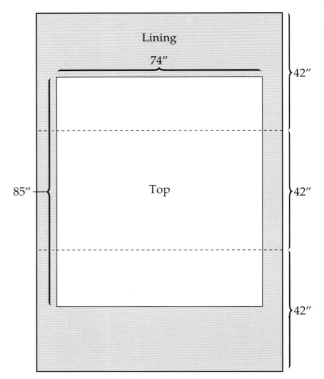

FIG. 8.4 *Utilizing lining with horizontal seam*

QUEEN- AND KING-SIZED QUILTS

The seam that joins the lining pieces can be centered down the middle in a twin or double lining. However, the larger-size quilts need 2¹/₂ to 3 widths of fabric. These seams should be evenly spaced, having one complete width down the center and balancing the remainder evenly on both sides.

If the quilt is 88" by 94", the lining should be 92" by 98" to allow for contraction. Use one-width of fabric down the center. Figure this as 42" wide after seams and selvages are subtracted. Since the lining needs to be 92" wide, subtract 42" from 92": You will need 50" of width. If this width is divided by two, you find you need 25" more on each side of the center piece (Figure 8.5).

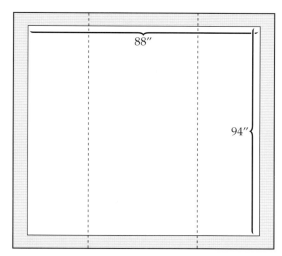

FIG. 8.6 *Vertical seam*

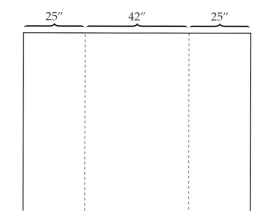

FIG. 8.5 *Lining construction*

We now know we need three lengths of fabric to accommodate the width of the quilt. Each length should be 2³/₄ yards (98" by 36"). Two and three quarter yards by 3 lengths is 8¹/₄ yards for the lining (Figure 8.6).

Try figuring this same quilt using horizontal seams. You should find only ³/₈-yard difference. In this case, preference for vertical or horizontal seams is the deciding factor as to which method to use (Figure 8.7).

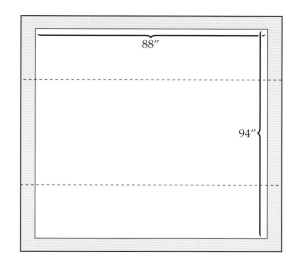

FIG. 8.7 *Horizontal seam*

One last example for a king-size quilt: The quilt measures 100" by 120". The lining needs to be 104" by 124". To figure for vertical seams, divide the width of the quilt by 42" to see how many lengths of fabric are needed. This is 104" by 42" = 3 lengths. The quilt length plus contraction allowances is divided by 36": 124" by 36" = 3¹/₂ yards. Three lengths times 3¹/₂ yards is 10¹/₂ yards (Figure 8.8).

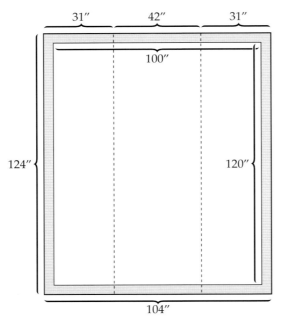

FIG. 8.8 Vertical seams

If batting needs to be joined to get the needed size, figure for the yardage needed the same way. Refer to Chapter 6 for information on splicing batting together to get larger pieces for king quilts when not available in that size.

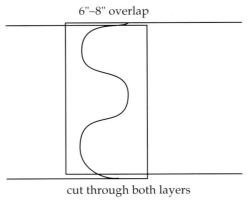

FIG. 8.10 Splicing batting together

To figure for horizontal seams, divide the length by 42": 124" by 42" = 3 widths needed. Each length should be 104" long, or 104" divided by 36" = 3 yards. Three yards times 3 lengths is 9 yards. By using horizontal seams instead of vertical ones, you can save 1¹/₂ yards of fabric (Figure 8.9).

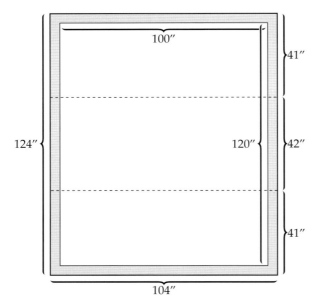

FIG. 8.9 Horizontal seams

LAYERING

O nce the batting has been chosen, the top has been squared and pressed well, and the quilting designs have been carefully marked onto the quilt top, you are ready to put the layers together and pin baste. Do not bind the quilt before quilting. If you have ever stretched and basted a quilt on the floor by the old, traditional methods, you are going to appreciate the method presented here. No more aching back or sore knees.

Create a work surface that is about 3 feet wide and 5 to 6 feet long. This could be a sheet of plywood, a counter top, the dining room table, etc. Avoid using ping-pong and pool tables, as they are too wide and the lining fabric will not be stretched properly. To lessen back strain, raise the height of the table by placing stacks of books under the table legs to achieve a comfortable height (usually waist height). If you do not have a table to work on, cut a piece of $^3/_4$" plywood 3 feet by 6 feet, varnish it, and place it on two sawhorses that you have made to be your working height. This is an inexpensive way to get a good working surface, and it can be taken down and put out of the way when not needed.

Measure the length and width of the table to find the center points on all four sides Mark these centers with drafting tape. A student once suggested placing the tape over a toothpick so you can feel the bump through the layers of fabric throughout the process. Excellent idea!

FIG. 9.1 Marking centers of table

Once the lining is sewn together and pressed well to remove all creases, fold in half lengthwise, wrong sides together. Also note the crosswise center of the lining. Place the folds on the tape guidelines.

FIG. 9.2 Centered lining

Unfold to one thickness, wrong side facing up. Allow the excess to hang over the edges of the table. The center of the lining should run down the center of the table.

FIG. 9.3 Opening lining

Smooth the fabric over the table top. Using binder clips or any strong clamp that will fit your surface, stretch the lining over the table top. Begin by clamping one end using two or three clamps. Then lightly stretch and clamp the opposite end. After clamping both ends, stretch and clamp the sides. Try to keep the lining as centered as possible. Use as many clamps as necessary to keep the lining smooth and taut, but do not stretch it so tightly that it distorts the grainline of the fabric. You should be able to run your hand over the fabric and see no movement or crawling.

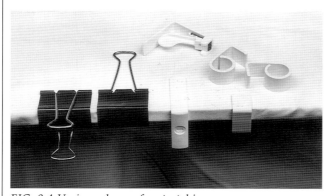

FIG. 9.4 Various clamps for stretching

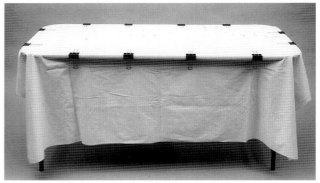

FIG. 9.5 Stretched lining

Stretching controls any fullness in the lining fabric before going to the machine so the feed dogs will not make any tucks and puckers. This virtually eliminates all distortion and tucks on the lining side.

Note: If the quilt or project is too small to clamp on one or more sides, use masking or drafting tape to tape the edges when stretching. This is sufficient for blocks, small wall quilts, and baby quilts.

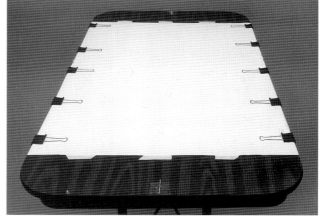

FIG. 9.6 Tape stretching

Next, fold the batting in half lengthwise. Make sure it is smooth and free of fold lines and stretch marks. If polyester batting is distorted from packaging, place it in the clothes dryer, on the very lowest heat setting, with a damp hand towel and tumble it for 10 to 15 minutes. This should soften and remove the fold lines. Use steam to remove the fold lines from natural fiber batts.

Lay the fold at the center placement guides on top of the lining. Unfold the batting so that it hangs over the edges of the table. Smooth it out gently without stretching it. The lining and batting should be the same size, and should be 2"–4" larger than the quilt top.

FIG. 9.9 *Layering completed*

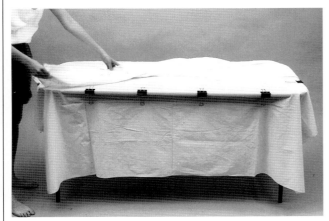

FIG. 9.7 *Positioning batting*

Be careful not to stretch the quilt top; just smooth it gently over the batting. If the top was well pieced and properly pressed, it will smooth evenly. If not, there might be extra fullness in some places, tightness in others. Do not force these areas to lie flat, since that will cause distortion in other areas, especially the borders. You will need to work the fullness in as you quilt that area.

Now you are ready for the quilt top. Fold the quilt top in half lengthwise, right sides together. Center the fold over the center placement guides (toothpicks), and open it so that it hangs over the edges of the table. The three layers—lining, batting, and quilt top—should now be centered and stacked.

FIG. 9.8 *Centering quilt top*

BASTING TOOLS

You will need an abundant supply of #1, nickel-plated safety pins to pin baste the layers together. These pins are 1" long and have a fine tip that will leave a very small hole in the cloth. Large pins are easier to close, but they put damaging holes in the fabrics. Safety pins are used because they stay in the quilt as it is rolled and re-rolled throughout the quilting process. Nickel-plated pins are preferred because brass pins can rust, and they may leave a black mark in the fabric where they are inserted. If you are unsure if your pins are rust-proof or not, place a few in a wet piece of fabric and let the fabric dry. If they rust, do not use them in your quilt. If you can find them in bulk, #0 pins are a little smaller and finer. At least 350 safety pins are needed to layer a double-size quilt, 500 or more for a king. Do not skimp on the number of pins that you use.

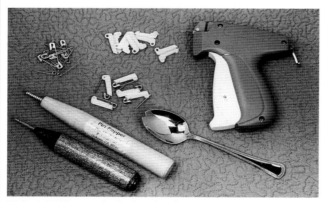

FIG. 9.10 *New tools for basting layers together*

A wonderful new product has become available recently called "Safety Pin Grips." These are butterfly-shaped pieces of plastic that snap over the top of the safety pin and act as a little handle on the top of the pin. This gives your fingers more grip with less pressure, and makes the safety pins very easy and comfortable to work with. Check with your local quilt shop for these.

Another interesting tool to show up is the Quilt Tack™. This is similar to the tool that puts hang tags on garments. You insert the needle through the layers of the quilt, then pull the trigger and the tab is inserted. This tool is a real help to people whose hands are weaker and have trouble handling the safety pins.

Regular basting will not hold up to machine quilting. It allows the layers to shift and bunch when packaging and re-rolling. Also, it tends to get caught in the foot as you sew, and it's difficult to remove after stitching over the threads with many rows of machine stitching. Remember: The pinning and layering process is 90% of the success of machine quilting. Make sure that whatever method you choose, the quilt layers are tightly secured together to prevent shifting. If you have not layered well, you will have endless trouble as you attempt to quilt on the machine.

On thin, cotton-type batting, place the pins 3"–4" apart. If a thicker, more wiry polyester-type batting is used, place the pins much closer together (approximately 2"–3" apart). The more you can control the layers from shifting during the layering process, the easier the quilting will be.

When pinning the layers together, start in the center and work toward the corners. Try to avoid pinning across seam lines that will be ditch stitched or across any design lines. Place pins so that you can maneuver around them. Again, do not stretch and force any fabric to lie flat if it doesn't do so naturally. Ease the fullness in as you pin.

FIG 9.11 *Safety pin basting*

Close the safety pins as you go. New tools such as the notched spoon, the Pin Popper™ and the Kwik Klip™ are invaluable for closing the pins. These tools hold the fabric down while the pin is going through the layers, then the point comes up into a groove that holds it secure, allowing you to simply push the top of the pin over the point and close it. No more sore and bloody fingers!

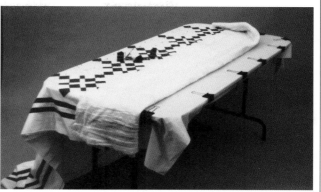

FIG. 9.13 Restretching lining after repositioning

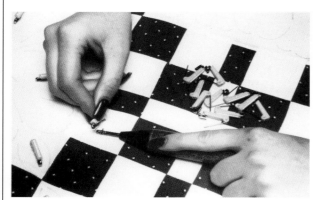

FIG 9.12 Closing pins with the Kwik Klip

Do not try to eliminate any of these steps. Once the entire quilt is pin basted, turn it over and run your hands over the surface. If any fullness backs up against a pin, you may need to unpin that area and restretch and repin to eliminate possible problems. This procedure also keeps your quilts from stretching and becoming distorted while machine quilting.

Once the table top area has been pinned, remove the clamps from all sides of the table. Slide the quilt layers to one side, so that all but 2" of the pinned area is hanging off one side of the table. On the opposite side of the table, reach under to find the lining. Gently stretch the lining only, using the pinned area to stretch against. Reclamp the lining onto the edge opposite from the pinned area. Then stretch the ends and reclamp them. Do not clamp the pinned side. The weight from the pins will give enough resistance to keep the lining stretched. Reposition the batting and the quilt top, smooth, and start to pin the layers together from the pinned area to the opposite side. Repeat this process until that side is completely pinned. Repeat the process for the other side of the quilt, then again for the ends. You might want to rotate the quilt so that the ends are now placed on the length of the table to make it faster to stretch and pin baste.

PACKAGING

Whether you are quilting a whole quilt or quilt-as-you-go sections, the following techniques apply. I have two rules I follow when preparing to quilt: First, never turn a quilt under the machine. Turning causes distortion from pushing the batting in too many directions. Besides this, it is very difficult, if not impossible, to successfully turn a large quilt and get all the excess through the 9" opening of your sewing machine. Second, have only half of the quilt under the machine at any time; begin stitching on the center line, and once it is completed, move to the right. Continually unrolling the roll that is in the machine decreases it, making the quilting easier. Once that side is done, the quilt will be turned end-to-end and the process repeated for the other side. More detail on this will be given in the individual quilt section.

The first step in packaging is to lay the quilt right side up on a table. Work from the center line or row of blocks to the right. Fold the left side of the quilt up to the center line or row to within 2" from the line. The left side of the quilt will be supported by the table. Roll the right side of the quilt as tight as you can, also to within 2" from the center line. This is the side that goes through the machine and needs to be rolled tight so that it will fit. (Again, batting will make a difference in what size quilt you will be able to handle with this packaging process. You may need to quilt-as-you-go in sections.)

If the roll wants to unroll, it will create problems when you try to manipulate the fabric to do the quilting lines. Bicycle pant-leg clips, also known as Quilters Clips™, will hold the roll in place. These clips are made of spring steel and go around the large roll to secure it. Be sure that you get the oval clips, not the round ones. They stay in place much better. You will also find various clips made of cut PVC pipe, or different plastic clips such as Jaws™. Look for clips that are the size that correspond with the size of your quilt. Covering the metal clips with twill tape will keep them from sliding and scratching your machine. You will need four to 12 of these clips for large quilts.

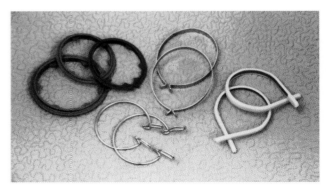

FIG. 10.1 *Various clips for quilt roll*

Place them down the length of the quilt, using enough to control the quilt. Use the clips on the left side if you find that it is trying to come unfolded. An added bonus to the clips is that the roll does not collapse as the length of the quilt extends behind the machine. When unrolling to the right for the next quilting line, you can unroll within the clips; they do not have to be removed each time. This speeds up the process immensely (Figure 10.2).

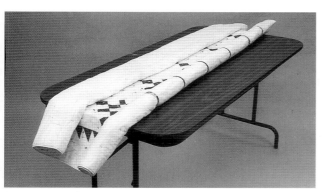

FIG. 10.2 *Packaging process*

Do a zigzag (accordion) fold from the end, making a compact package to put in your lap. It will automatically unfold as you work (Figure 10.3).

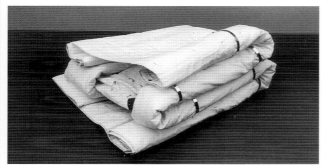

FIG. 10.3 *Accordion pleated*

Sit down at the machine with the package in your lap. Place the quilt under the machine at the beginning of the line, and insert the needle. Adjust the quilt in your lap. Unroll or unfold a couple of times and "punch" it up to rest on your chest so that the quilt is going down into the machine, not dragging up from your lap. Now you are ready to stitch. If the quilt is too large to hold in your lap, throw it over your left shoulder.

FIG. 10.4 *Lap position for straight-set quilt*

If your quilting lines are diagonal in the quilt, use the same packaging technique, but roll the right side in from the corner point, and fold the left side from the opposite corner point. Instead of folding the length of the quilt into a square package, throw it over your left shoulder and feed it into the machine. (When folded diagonally, the quilt package tends to fall apart.) Use your shoulder and arm to keep the sides rolled, and feed into the machine consistently.

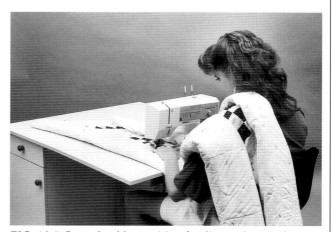

FIG. 10.5 *Over shoulder position for diagonal set quilt*

If you are working with the quilt on your shoulder, you may find that it becomes rather heavy and hot. You might consider rigging up a system that supports the quilt off your body. An idea could be to take an 18" cafe curtain rod and, using a rope tied to either end, suspend it from a hook in the ceiling above your shoulder. This would allow the quilt to be in the right position, but off your shoulder. You can also get up and walk away, then come back with it in the correct position, starting right back where you left off.

Tip: Do not wear a cotton or other natural fiber blouse or shirt when doing this, or the quilt will stick to you, making progress difficult. Instead, wear a slick polyester blouse that will shed the cotton fabrics.

This is the general packaging process. Each quilt will have a specific order in which things need to be done. Now you know all you need to start learning machine quilting techniques.

STRAIGHT-LINE QUILTING

The easiest and most common form of machine quilting is quilting in the ditch. This is not a decorative technique, but more of a structural technique. Many quilt tops do not need fancy quilting on the surface of the quilt. If the piecing design is very strong or if the fabric pattern is busy and predominant, the quilting generally won't show over it. Stitching in the ditch is a functional way to secure the three layers together. This method is also used to anchor between the blocks before doing surface quilting within the blocks. This makes the quilt much more stable and makes it easier to control under the machine's foot (Figure 11.1). Grid quilting, another common form of machine quilting, adds surface texture to strong designs without adding pattern. Unlike ditch quilting, grid quilting gives an overall quilted effect that can enhance many quilts. Both of these forms of quilting are done using the walking foot.

PREPARING TO DITCH QUILT

The ditch method is good for beginning machine quilters. It is done with the walking foot to stitch long, straight lines. This foot does use a feeding system, so care must be taken to prevent shifting layers. Remember that when planning the order of the quilting process, you do not want to turn the quilt under the machine, and only half of the bulk is under the machine at any time.

The ditch is created by pressing the seam allowance to one side, leaving a high side and a low side to the seam. Pressing is a very important part of ditch quilting. If you have not pressed your blocks extremely well

during construction, then try press the seams joining the blocks together once the top is finished, you will encounter trouble when quilting the seams.

Press the seams to one side, working from the fabric front, so that there are no little pleats or extra fabric that prevents the needle from getting as close to the seam as possible. If the pressing is not done well, you can experience quite a bit of distortion throughout the entire quilt when pulling the seam apart to stitch. Make sure that the blocks lay perfectly flat and smooth before putting together the top, and that the top lays flat and square before layering.

To identify where the ditch is, rub your thumb over the seam. You will feel a ridge. The ridge represents the side of the seam with the three thicknesses of fabric. The low side of the ridge is only the single thickness of the quilt block. When ditch quilting, the needle should always be on the low side, just rubbing the ridge edge as you are stitching. When the seam is stitched and the fabric relaxes, the stitching is completely hidden in the fold.

FIG. 11.1 *Needle position for ditch quilting*

A common problem that every new quilter needs to deal with is imperfect piecing. When ditch quilting, you need to keep the stitching in the ditch at all times. You do not want to see the stitches away from the seam. However, if the intersections of the block pieces or sashing strips do not butt perfectly, there is a tendency to aim from one ditch to another, allowing the stitching to show on top of the fabric where the seams do not butt.

Looking at Figure 11.2, you see a seam that is perfectly butted. The top seam is pressed to the left and the bottom seam is pressed to the right. You will begin the seam by stitching on the right side of the seam on the top section, and as you approach the intersection, you will find that the ditch is on the left side of the seam. Because the seam is evenly butted, you will simply merge to the left side of the seam in the bottom section, again making sure that the needle is rubbing the ridge of the seam. Because the seam is a continuous straight line, the stitching stays hidden totally in the ditch.

FIG. 11.3 *A poorly butted seam*

Start again at the top seam and stitch down the right side of the seam. When you come to the intersection, stop the needle where the horizontal and vertical seams intersect. Take one stitch there, then lift the needle and the presser bar, and move the quilt to the left just enough so that you can place the needle in the intersection of the horizontal and bottom vertical seam. Resume stitching in the left hand ditch of the bottom seam. You will have a tiny stair-step stitch laying in the horizontal seam at this point. This is preferable to seeing stitches on the top of the piece aiming from one seam to another. If you have to make this adjustment very many times, you will learn to clean up your piecing skills. This exercise does slow down the process of ditch quilting, but the finished look of the quilt is well worth the effort. Practice doing this on a sample block a couple of times.

FIG. 11.2 *A perfectly butted seam*

If the intersection is not perfectly butted, as in Figure. 11.3, there is a gap or overlapped area that needs to be dealt with when stitching through the intersection.

Before you start to learn the stitching process, become familiar with where your eyes need to be when working with a walking foot. Mount your walking foot onto your machine, then lower the presser bar so that the foot is sitting on the feed dogs. Now lower the needle into the machine. There is generally a line or small opening on the front of the foot, between the toes, that denotes where the center of the foot is. Look at the needle and see if it lines up perfectly with this line. It more than likely does not. Now think of how you sew. We generally align the foot with the fabric. If you are ditch quilting, and you place the foot on the fabric and align the marking of the foot exactly with the seam, but the needle is not also in line with the foot, where is the stitching going to be? It won't be in the ditch! The other problem is that if you are looking at the line and the seam, and adjust the quilt so that they remain in alignment, you are again taking the needle out of position because it is following the marking by $1/4$". Looking at the foot is not the preferred method of ditch quilting.

You are going to want to start training your eyes to look at the needle, and make sure that the needle is always rubbing the seam, every stitch of the way (as shown in Figure 11.1). If you have trouble seeing the needle, try sitting higher above the machine so that you look directly down on the foot and can see the needle going in and out of the fabric, and/or cut a wider opening between the toes of your walking foot to make an open toe foot, as discussed in Chapter 2. If you are ditch quilting properly, you are looking at the needle every stitch of the way, disregarding where the foot is in relation to the seam. This is awkward at first because we are still in a sewing mode at this time. You are now going to start learning to "hand quilt with an electric needle."

Before starting any project, make it a habit to test your machine on a sample of the fabric and batting that will be used in the quilt. Once this sandwich is made, quilt a few rows of stitches, checking that the tension and stitch length are correct. You are looking for perfect, balanced tension that shows no loops of bobbin thread on the top surface, and no loops of top thread on the lining. Adjust your tensions accordingly (refer to page 12 for more information). The desirable stitch length is similar to the length you like in hand quilting, about 8–12 stitches per inch. Remember, a stitch that is too short will perforate and weaken the fibers, and can cause tearing when stress is applied to the quilt. A stitch that is too long will break when stress is applied. When running sample stitches, check on the back to be sure that the stitches are consistently the same length. If they are erratic, your walking foot may not be mounted properly, or you are using your hands too much, not allowing the foot to do all the feeding, which will be addressed later.

ANCHORING THE LAYERS TOGETHER

When ditch or grid quilting a project, anchoring is easy to do, and allows the layers to remain straight and free of distortion. Stitch the anchor lines first when starting to quilt. They are the very center seamlines in the quilt, both lengthwise and crosswise. (If there is no seam in the very center of the quilt, move to the first seam to the right of the center.) You quilt these two lines first so that the quilt cannot shift and distort as you continue on quilting the other lines. If you fail to do this, the layers will tend to shift in the direction the foot is pushing, causing the border and corner to get out of square. This is a common problem for beginners.

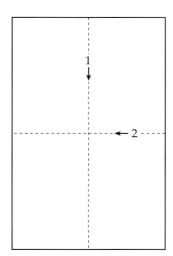

FIG. 11.4 Anchoring

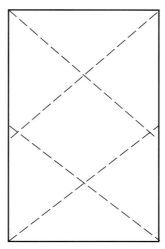

FIG. 11.5b Anchoring a rectangular diagonal set

When deciding on which seam to anchor first, consider where the grainlines of the batting and lining are. As discussed in Chapters 6 and 8, the lining and batting both have lengthwise and crosswise grainlines. Try to keep both the batting and lining grainlines running in the same direction. If you have the lengthwise grainline of the batting and lining going the length of the quilt, you will quilt the lengthwise center seam first. If the lengthwise grainline is running across the width of the quilt, you would quilt the center crosswise seam first. Always quilt the seam that runs with the batting and lining lengthwise grain first to eliminate possible stretching and distortion.

If the quilt top is a square and a diagonal set, you will anchor the layers by quilting from one corner to the opposite corner diagonally, then repeating the process on remaining corners. This will make an "X" across the quilt. If the quilt is longer than it is wide, you will make two "X's" so that all four corners are stitched (Figure 11.5b).

Do not start the quilting line in the center of the quilt and stitch the top half, then start in the center again and stitch the lower half. This can cause heavy distortion in the center of the quilt, and you will be working twice as hard to achieve the same thing.

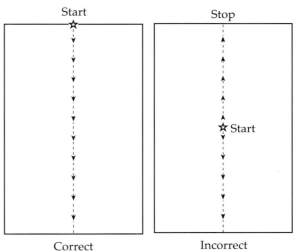

FIG. 11.6
Correct stitching direction

FIG. 11.7
Incorrect stitching direction

Read through all the instructions before beginning, and try the method first on the practice block or quilt. This will give you a chance to master the skills and techniques before moving on to a larger project.

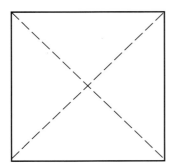

FIG. 11.5a Anchoring a square diagonal set

DITCH QUILTING THEORY

Begin quilting on the center seam that applies to the suggestion on page 82. Position the block or quilt so that the very center lengthwise seam, or the first seam to the right of the center, is exposed. Remember, when packaging a larger project, the left side is folded to within 2" of the seam and the right side is rolled as tight as you can get it and clamped with bicycle clips. Accordion pleat the quilt from the bottom up and place the top edge under the machine. Review Chapter 10 for this technique.

If you are on the raw edge of the block, hold both the top and bobbin threads tightly in your left hand as you begin to stitch.

FIG. 11.8 *Holding threads on edge*

If there is a border or sashing strip around the block, the stitching will begin inside the border at the border seamline.

FIG. 11.9 *Holding threads inside border*

Bring the bobbin thread to the surface before beginning to stitch by taking one complete stitch, either manually with the hand wheel or by using the automatic needle-up position on newer machines. Make sure that the take up lever is in its highest position when you stop. This assures that the top thread is no longer wrapped around the bobbin shuttle and that it can be easily pulled to the top. Move the fabric over slightly and pull on the top thread from both sides of the needle hole. The bobbin thread should appear up through the hole. Pull it through so that you can hold onto it as you begin the stitching. While holding the threads, insert the needle into the ditch, and lower the walking foot.

The thread tails need to be locked off before starting to quilt. Stitching in place and back-stitching are not the best methods for locking the thread into the fabric. Because the nylon is so slippery, it will slip out of these stitches. Instead, make a $1/4$" line of very tiny stitches buried in the ditch to keep the thread from creeping out. To do this, put your stitch length on $1/2$" or about 24–30 stitches per inch. Stitch for $1/4$" distance at this setting. These stitches are so small that they cannot pull out. Once this is done, move the length regulator to the number that you found suitable on your sample, generally $2^1/2$"–3", or 8–12 stitches per inch. When the stitching is locked off, clip the thread tails even with the surface of the fabric. This method keeps you from having to weave the threads back into the batting or tying them off. This locking system is critical when using nylon thread.

As you begin to stitch at the normal length stitch, do not help the machine more than is necessary by pushing, shoving and pulling the fabric through the foot. This will only lead to distortion and tucks. The walking foot is designed to feed the top layer of fabric evenly with the lining as it is pulled through the feed dogs. Train your hands to work with the fabric and the foot. Do not push and pull.

GALAXY

Designed, machine appliquéd, and quilted by Betty Gilliam, Stillwater, OK;
nylon and Sulky rayon threads; Hobbs Heirloom® premium cotton batting
64" x 69"

ORIENTAL POPPY

Adapted from a 1871 quilt pattern and a 1937 quilt made by Charlotte Jane Whitehill;
machine appliquéd by Nancy Hieronymus Barrett, Edmond, OK;
machine quilted by Harriet Hargrave using grid, free-motion, ditch, outline,
and echo quilting techniques; nylon and cotton thread;
Hobbs Heirloom® premium cotton batting
82" x 82

OHIO ROSE

Machine appliquéd and quilted by Jean Lohmar,
Galesburg, IL using echo, stipple, and free-motion
quilting techniques; nylon and metallic threads;
Fairfield Cotton Classic® batting
91" x 103"

WITH ALL MY HEART

Designed and machine quilted by Mary Pilger Lambert, Eureka, IL using stipple, grid, channel, and free-motion quilting techniques; nylon thread; Hobbs Heirloom® premium cotton batting
86" x 102"

WHIG ROSE

1920's quilt; two lengths of fabric, machine quilted in ¹/₂" grid then joined using the quilt-as-you-go method; appliqués were stitched by hand onto quilted fabric; binding by machine in ditch; cotton thread and batting; collection of Harriet Hargrave
72" x 80"

COURTHOUSE STEPS CRIB QUILT

Late 1800's quilt; machine quilted with hanging diamond grid quilting; cotton thread and batting; collection of Harriet Hargrave
32" x 49"

LANCASTER ROSE

*Machine appliquéd and quilted by
Harriet Hargrave using free-motion
quilting; Mountain Mist®
100% polyester batting
45" x 45"*

Boston Commons Back

BOSTON COMMONS VARIATION

Machine pieced and quilted by Sandy Espenschied, Atlanta, GA; nylon thread; Mountain Mist® 100% natural cotton batting 70" x 70"

OHIO ROSE

*Machine appliquéd and quilted by
Harriet Hargrave using free-motion, ditch, echo,
and grid quilting techniques; nylon thread;
Mountain Mist® 100% natural batting
62" x 62"*

Remember: Keep your fingers in front of the foot, assisting it in easing any fullness in the top layer only.

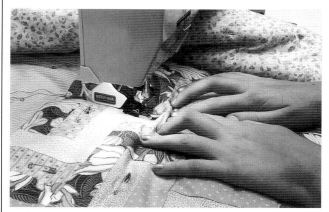

FIG. 11.10 Feeding fabric to walking foot

You will often see that the top layer wants to push ahead a bit, and when you come to a seam, a small tuck will appear. This can be eliminated by feeding that excess fabric to the foot while stitching the length of the seam. To do this, place your thumbs against the pins in the area, while your fingers gently push any fullness—of the top only—toward the foot (Figure 11.10). You will only be working with the 1"-2" area right in front of the needle. Be careful that you do not also push the batting and lining. As you stitch, allow the walking foot to gently pull this excess fabric into itself. As it does this, it will evenly ease out the fullness within the stitches. There should be no gathering, tucks, or pleats. Gently walk your fingers just in front of the walking foot for the entire length of the seam. Use your fingers to position any extra quilt top fabric in front of the foot.

Stretching the seam in front of and behind the foot to prevent tucks from being sewn in will only distort the quilt when finished. When the batting is stretched and then stitched, it will try to rebound to its original shape, creating dips and valleys at the cross-seams, and fluting at the edges. If you follow the guidelines for feeding the excess fullness, the quilt will lie flat without tucks or distortion. Allow the walking foot to work for you, easing the fullness in gradually and consistently the full length of the seam.

If you are experiencing problems seeing, adjust the height of your chair. Retrain your eyes to watch the needle and know where it is going with every stitch. If you watch the foot and compensate for the position of the foot in relation to the seam, the needle will not be where it needs to be at any given time. If you watch the needle, you have the control to adjust the seam to accommodate the needle's position. Raising the height of your chair will eliminate glare from the machine light, and will allow you to see the hole where the needle is stitching. (Refer to page 10 for more information on chair height.)

As you approach the last ¼" of the seam, slow down and start to decrease the stitch length. Be sure that the last ¼" of the seam is made up of very tiny stitches (24–30 stitches to the inch) to lock off the end of the stitching.

Now go back and examine the seam for quality and technique problems. The stitching should be on the low side of the ditch at all times. You do not want to see stitches on the fold of the high side. The stitches should be consistently the same length.

Note: Often the walking foot will hang up on bulky seam allowances. If this happens, you will see a few tiny stitches in that area. When you feel this happen with your foot, stop, lift the foot slightly, and set it down again. This will release the fabric that gets snagged under the foot. If this happens a lot, you can shave a bit of the plastic off of the center back feeder on the walking foot. This small piece of plastic can get stuck on the bulk of the seam allowances and "high center" the rest of the foot. By shaving some of it off, it does not catch as often. (See Chapter 2.)

There should be no gathers, tucks, or stretched areas along the seam. Finally, the area where seams cross each other should be exactly perpendicular and square. If the line sags below a straight line, the fabric has been allowed to push ahead, and the quilt will look distorted when finished. If any of these things happen, go back and practice the feeding technique.

DITCH QUILTING PRACTICES

Practice these techniques on a block such as an Ohio Star that is pieced with many seams, or use a large square made of many small squares sewn together. A small quilt would also be suitable for this exercise. You will learn to stay in the ditch, and feed the fabric properly while using the walking foot. Follow the techniques previously given, and ditch quilt the center lengthwise seam from the top edge (or top border seam) through to the bottom edge (or bottom border seam). Handle the block as if it were a full-size quilt. Do not turn the block or quilt.

Next, quilt the center crosswise seamline. Refold and reroll so that the center crosswise seam is exposed. This is the second anchor seam. Stitch from the side edge (or border seam) to the opposite side edge (or border seam). If you are not feeding properly, a tuck will appear as you cross the first anchor line. Again, do not stretch the fabric to eliminate it. Remove the seam and try again. This time, ease the fullness up to the foot as you go. Finally, examine the seam for quality. This completes the anchoring seams, which will help prevent the layers from shifting throughout the rest of the quilting process.

Once you have anchored the quilt, you are ready to continue with the remaining seams. Repackage the quilt, once again lengthwise. You will continue to stitch the seams that are to the right of the center until you reach the border.

Each stitching line will begin at the top border or edge and continue down through the anchor line to the bottom border or edge. Lock off the stitches at the beginning and end of every seam. Unroll the roll to the next line, fold up the left side more, and quilt the next line to the right from the top border or edge to the bottom border or edge. Continue until the side is completed (Figure 11.11).

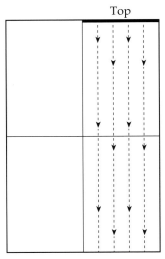

FIG. 11.11 *Stitching each line right of center*

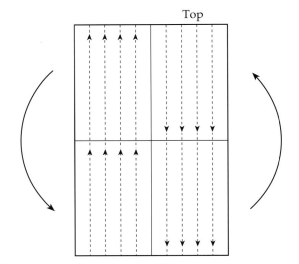

FIG. 11.12 *Stitching opposite side*

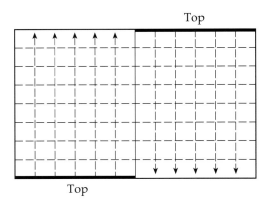

FIG. 11.13 *Stitching cross seams*

Repackage the quilt, but this time the roll will consist of the unquilted, lengthwise seams, and the fold on the left will be the previously quilted area. We have now turned the quilt end for end, so that the true bottom of the quilt is in the top position. Repeat the above instructions, working to the right, until all the lengthwise lines are stitched (Figure 11.12).

The crosswise seams are quilted next. The quilting becomes easier because the quilt is now well secured. You will now cross the lengthwise quilted seams. Continue to work with the walking foot to eliminate all tucks at the seam crossings. Repackage the quilt so that the crosswise seams are ready to be quilted. Quilt from the center out to the right, top to bottom, until all seams are quilted. Rotate the quilt so that the other side is now on your right (top) and repeat (Figure 11.13).

Note: I treat the seam that attaches the border onto the top as one of the seams to be quilted in the above order, instead of trying to quilt it in a square after all the rest of the quilt is quilted. (The borders are added to the top before the quilt is layered.) This eliminates having to turn corners with the foot, which can push the batting slightly, causing the corner to stretch or cup up. Double-check your work to make sure you are keeping the quilt square and straight. After reviewing the section on free-motion quilting you will be ready to quilt the borders.

Once you are finished, check your project for quality. Look for adequate, small lock-off stitches at the beginning and end of each line of stitching. All seams should be straight and free of tucks and puckers. If there is distortion of the fabric between stitching lines, you need to improve your technique when working with the foot and the feeding system. Check the back of the quilt and make sure that all stitches are the same size (within reason) and that there are no tucks or gathering on the backing fabric. All of these small details need attention if you want to master machine quilting. Trim the edges, square the corners, and bind. You are now well on your way to finishing all those tops in the closet!

The Rail Fence quilt pictured below is just one example of a pattern that is perfect for a first ditch quilting project. Individual blocks are sewn together into rows, then the rows are sewn together. These joining seams make a perfect place to ditch quilt, giving the quilt a puffy texture and appearance, and stabilizing the layers. There is no need to add additional quilting to the surface if you have chosen your batting wisely.

Ditch quilting is often used alone, as with the Rail Fence quilt. It is more often used to secure the layers together before adding surface quilting designs using the free-motion techniques discussed in Chapter 13.

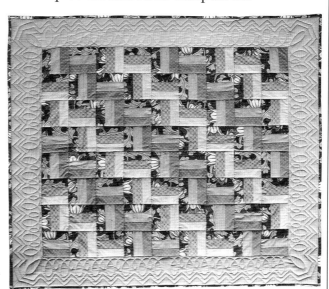

FIG. 11.14 Rail Fence quilt

FIG. 11.15 Diagonal grid quilting

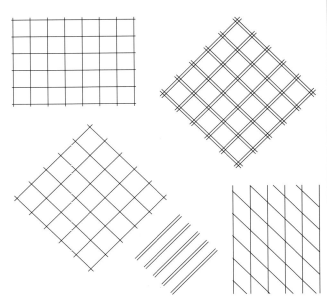

FIG. 11.16 Various grid patterns

GRID QUILTING TECHNIQUES
Grid quilting is simply stitching straight or diagonal lines at equal intervals over the top of the pattern, regardless of design (Figure 11.15). It is a very functional type of quilting that adds a wonderful relief effect to the overall quilt. Grid quilting is often seen on antique quilts since it is a fast method of hand quilting. Strong and durable, it is a marvelous way to do extensive, close quilting on the machine for quilts such as Log Cabin, Pineapple and other old, traditional quilt patterns. The grids can either be straight, diagonal, double diagonal, hanging diamonds, or any combination you choose as illustrated in Figure 11.16. You will probably need to mark the lines on the quilt top to keep the lines straight and parallel. The rug canvas method described on page 29 is useful in helping you place the lines on the quilt top. Check Chapter 4 for other ways to mark parallel lines.

Many of your quilts can be quilted using straight lines. If these instructions are followed and care is taken in your quilting, you will have beautifully quilted quilts with a minimum of learning time. If straight lines do not enhance your quilt enough, continue to the next chapter to learn the magic of free-motion quilting.

FREE-MOTION QUILTING TECHNIQUES

Free-motion quilting will open up a new world to you. I have no doubt that it will become your favorite method of machine quilting. It requires quite a bit of practice to master, but you will find the time well spent when you are able to reproduce beautiful quilting designs in minutes. What freedom you are allowed when the presser foot is removed! You can go forward, backward, side-to-side, in circles—anywhere you want to go—without ever turning the quilt. Specific techniques and detailed instructions are given for each method.

FREE-MOTION EXERCISES—PLAIN FABRIC

After years of teaching machine quilting, I have found students have the most fun experimenting and playing with free-motion techniques. However, free-motion quilting is not instant gratification. It will take many hours of practice to master the techniques.

Before you begin practicing the designs, first start thinking about laying a solid foundation of ideas and thoughts of what the motion will be to create the patterns. Consider your sewing machine an extension of your arms and eyes. The machine must become a part of you, not just an awkward machine in your way. If you haven't cleaned and waxed the sewing surface of the machine, you will need to do so to keep the fabric gliding smoothly through the machine. If you have prewashed your backing fabric, treat it with a spray sizing or starch, putting a crisp finish back into the fabric. This will also assist in the ease of moving the fabric through the machine.

It is most helpful to have your sample practice blocks layered using 100% cotton batting because the layers stick together and eliminate the need for pinning. Your rhythm won't be broken by dodging pins or stopping to remove them.

If you put rubber filing fingers on the first three fingers of each hand, and each thumb, you will find that the rubber grip allows you to lighten your hand drag and enables you to move the fabric with a lot less pressure of the hands and stress to your shoulders and neck. You can purchase these rubber filing fingers in an office supply store. They have tiny tentacles on the surface that grab the fabric. Bare fingers tend to slip and slide, making you want to push down on the fabric more.

Put the darning foot on your machine, and drop or cover your feed dogs, whichever your machine requires. Check your manual if you are unsure how to do this. Because the feed dogs are dropped, no stitch length adjustment is necessary. The stitch length is controlled by the speed in which you move the fabric under the foot, and the speed of the machine.

Get in the habit of always bringing the bobbin thread to the surface of the fabric before beginning to stitch (Figure 12.1). Review the starting process on page 92 if you need help.

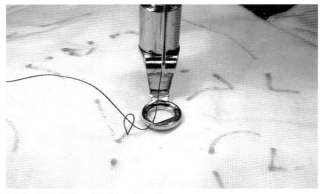

FIG. 12.1 *Bring bobbin thread to top*

Be sure that both threads are under the darning foot, not coming up through the hole. Having both threads on top prevents them from jamming and snarling on the underside. Next, lower the needle into the hole where the bobbin thread is, and lower the presser bar.

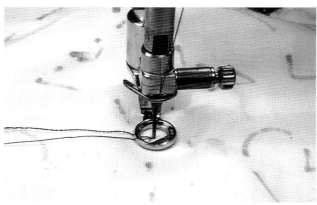

FIG. 12.2 *Re-insert needle*

Since no feeding is being done by the feed dogs, you will need to learn to move the fabric manually as you run the machine. This is where the concept "hand quilting with an electric needle" comes into play.

Your goal is to run the machine fairly fast. The faster you run the machine, the easier it is to develop accurate lines in your quilting, up to a point. If you run the machine too fast, you will tense up and work against yourself.

If you go too slowly, the stitches will be angular and possibly skipped. Try running your machine at various speeds while moving the fabric. Go as fast with the machine as you can while still breathing normally. If you start to tense up, slow down. If your stitches are long and erratic, speed up. The main thing is to get comfortable with the speed and RELAX. Practice on sample plain blocks.

Once you find a comfortable speed, try to keep it constant. Develop a rhythm with the motor speed of the machine. To do this, think about dancing. If you had your heart set on dancing the rumba, but the orchestra only played waltzes, you would have a difficult time dancing rumba steps while your ear was hearing waltzing rhythm. In terms of machine quilting, if the machine is running very fast, and your hands are moving very slow or erratic, your stitches will be very tiny and cluttered. If the machine is running very slow, and your hands want to go faster, the stitches will be very long and angular. If you are running the machine at various speeds, gunning and slowing down constantly, your hands cannot react to the speed changes, and the stitches will be always out of control. Do not gun the machine. **Tip:** If you find it hard to keep a constant speed with your foot control, consider placing a little block of wood behind the foot control, so that when you are at your optimum speed, the block will prevent any further changes. You might also want to try half motor speed if your machine has this feature. Often half speed, pushed all the way to the floor is just the right speed to start with. This also keeps you from going fast, then slow, then fast again. Erratic speed keeps your hands from developing a constant rhythm with the machine, and the quilting stitches will be ragged and uneven. Train your ear to listen to the sound of the motor, then memorize the sound of the speed that you are most comfortable with. When you hear the motor speed up or slow down, your ears tell your foot to correct itself and get back to the proper speed. As with dancing, when you hear the rhythm of the music, your feet follow in time. Practice "listening" by stitching on a plain block layered with cotton batting.

Next, you need to learn to control your hands. Become aware of how fast your hands should move the fabric under the needle to create the stitch length you want. You will ultimately want your free-motion stitches to match the stitches you made with the darning foot. If you ditch or grid quilt part of the quilt then finish up with free motion, you need to think about making all of the stitches the same length. This is where a lot of practice pays off. Take a breath and relax! Think of it as drawing with the needle. You want a steady, flowing motion with the fabric with the machine running at a constant speed.

Once you get a feel for the motion needed to move the fabric, start to move the fabric very slowly, side to side, keeping the machine at your favorite speed. Check to see what the stitch length looks like. Begin to speed up the motion of your hands, but always keep the machine at the same speed. You should start to see the stitch length get longer and longer until eventually you are creating a basting stitch. Your sample should look similar to Figure 12.3. This demonstrates how the stitch length is controlled totally by the motion of your hands, their consistency, and the speed of your machine. Refine the stitch length to the exact length you liked when using the walking foot. Eventually you will want all of your stitches to be the same length, regardless of the technique used. What you are really doing is measuring the length of the stitches with your eyes. You gauge their length by watching them as they develop. If they are too long, slow your hands down or speed up the machine. If they are too short, speed up your hands or slow the machine down. Remember, you are dancing with your machine, and rhythm is critical.

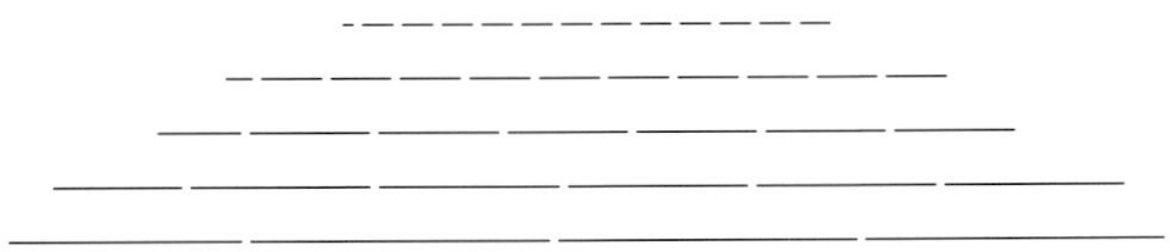

FIG. 12.3 Stitch length variations

Here are some exercises to develop your skills. Remember: Never turn the fabric, just glide it where you want it. Your hands need to be relaxed and your wrists kept up. Quilt with your fingertips, not your whole hand. This allows your fingers to gently walk the fabric where you want it. This position is similar to playing the piano (see Figure 12.4). The more your hands rest on the fabric, the more resistance there is to move the fabric against.

FIG. 12.4 Free-motion hand position

Use a gentle, sliding motion. An OUIJA® board is another example of how to position your hands on the fabric. Too much pressure will cause the fabric to drag, making jerky, uneven movements. Try resting your forearms or elbows on the edge of the table. Then you can lean into the work, removing the tension from your shoulders and back. Again, a good chair is critical here.

When stitching forward and backward as seen in the illustration below, don't worry if the lines are not straight. For now, you are only concerned with the stitch length quality. Keep going up and down until you are able to keep the stitches fairly accurate.

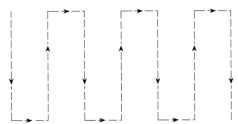
FIG. 12.5 Forward-backward exercises

Next, stitch side to side, left to right, back to the left, back to the right, etc. This will be foreign to you, as one generally does not sew sideways. Practice this until the stitches even out and become consistent.

FIG. 12.6 Side to side exercises

Now you are ready to do zigzags. This time, lock off the stitches at the beginning and end of each line. Do this by slowing the speed of the fabric, not the machine. You want to have $1/4$" of very tiny stitches at the beginning and end of every line as in ditch quilting. It may take practice to become accustomed to using different hand speeds while the machine is running at a constant speed. Repeat the lines shown below.

Lock
stitch

FIG. 12.7 Zigzag side to side

Curves are next. Try drawing "e" and "l" shapes as though practicing penmanship. Keep practicing until the curves are smooth and free of points and ragged edges. Also try loops, circles and anything else you can think of.

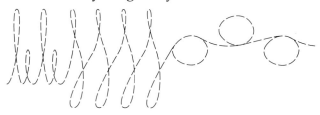

FIG. 12.8 Free-motion curves

Continue by drawing stars, hearts, your name, pictures or anything else that comes to mind. Do not draw these images on the fabric; rather, visualize them and reproduce what you see in your head. The freedom you experience is like soaring!

FIG. 12.9 Free-motion images

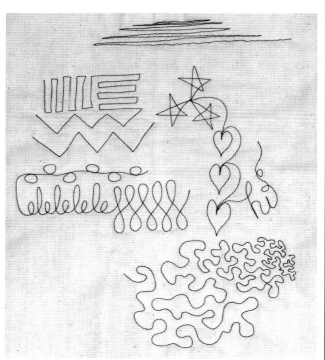

FIG. 12.10 Stitched sample

STIPPLE QUILTING

FIG. 12.11 Stipple quilting

Once you feel you have control of the fabric and the stitch length, you are ready to try stippling. Stipple quilting is a form of echo quilting when done by hand, but by machine it randomly fills in an entire area and creates a heavily quilted texture. Hand stippling is most often seen on antique counterpanes, but seldom on modern quilts because of the great amount of time needed to accomplish the process by hand.

Machine stippling, also known as meandering, is commonly used for background fill work. The stitching looks random at first glance, but when examined closely, you see that the lines never touch each other, they do not have points and angles, nor do they cross or look scribbled (Figure 12.11). They are very controlled, curly lines that systematically fill in both large and small areas with an abundance of texture. Stipple quilting can be very tiny or very large and open. Stipple techniques on the machine should not resemble echo quilting, but should appear totally random and free.

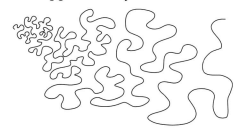

FIG. 12.12 Stipple quilting

As you were practicing the exercises earlier, you were mainly concerned about how to move the fabric under the needle to get where you wanted to go and still retain the shape you were trying to create. If you go back and do this again, you will find that you are no doubt looking at the needle or in the opening of the darning foot. This is a common problem. We are so trained to look at the foot and the needle when sewing, that we don't even think about it when quilting. We naturally stare at the needle. Now is the time to start breaking this habit. Look ahead of you, instead of in the foot opening. The smaller the darning foot, the easier it is to do this. You need to know where you are at, where you are going, and where you have been at all times. If you look ahead and all around, you can plan where you need to go and what you need to avoid before you get to it. When learning to stipple quilt, you need to constantly know what is coming at you, as you never want to cross any quilted lines. If you are looking in the foot, you will not only cross lines, but you'll tend to jerk away from a quilted line so that you don't touch it, creating angular, sloppy stitches. Practice quilting free-motion and not looking at the needle or in the foot for a while, then begin practicing stippling. Machine stippling is an excellent way to develop the skills of free-motion quilting, but it requires a lot of practice. You may need to sit with a piece of paper and doodle for a while to get the feel of the motion. Figure 12.12 shows a line drawing of stippling in various sizes. You may need to run the machine speed slower for very small stippling, and run your machine faster, moving your hand slower, for very large, open stippling.

When working a background with stippling, try not to get cornered. Plan the work so that it is very random and goes into every area continuously. Use the corners and points of the design to get in and out of the area. The photo in Figure 12.11 shows stippling in a variety of sizes. This combination is very effective when different textures are desired within one project.

FREE-MOTION DESIGN QUILTING

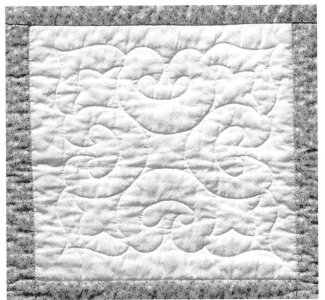

FIG. 12.13 Free-motion quilting

Borders and plain blocks are a perfect place to show off fancy quilting (see Figure 12.13). Free-motion quilting gives the machine quilter the maneuverability needed to reproduce intricate designs used by hand quilters. Almost any hand quilting design can be done using free-motion methods. It gives you access to small designs, sharp curves and intricate patterns often very difficult to achieve by hand. After practicing and experimenting, you will also find yourself ditch quilting shorter lines with your darning foot.

You should now have fairly adequate control of the fabric, and be quite comfortable with the machine's speed and your hands' motions. You are now ready to move on to a sample block with designs drawn on it.

Draw a variety of continuous curve patterns on the block from the designs in the back of this book. Free drawing is fairly easy, but it becomes more difficult when you are contained to a given line. When practicing the techniques don't get too involved with the stitch length quality at first. This whole process is much like learning to walk, chew gum, pat your head, and rub your tummy all at the same time. It is very difficult to train yourself to stay on the line, let alone be able to keep the stitches accurate. This will all develop with time and practice. For now, concentrate on the lines and your eye placement.

Learning to machine quilt on lines takes a lot of concentration. While practicing, give yourself plenty of uninterrupted quiet time, and don't expect to quilt perfectly at first.

FREE-MOTION EXERCISES— DESIGNS

Trace a stencil or design onto the fabric exactly as it will be stitched. Start at the star on the pattern and work through the numbers in order. Finger trace the design several times until you become familiar with the "road" the needle will take. Quilting this line for the first few times will be much like driving a very curvy road for the first time. You will be tempted to slow down at every curve to figure out where to go next. If you already know the road by finger tracing it a few times, you will be more apt to stay on the line.

This is where you really have to train your eyes not to look at the needle or in the opening of the foot. To further understand this principle, try this visualization exercise: Imagine yourself driving a car. You back out of the driveway, and as you start forward, you stare only at the hood ornament. If you do not look down the road, and you only stare at the hood ornament, where will you wind up? You have no control, and are flying blind. Now think of how you need to quilt. If you only stare at the needle, not the line ahead of you, you have no idea of where the lines goes and what you need to do to get the line and the needle in the same place. You must know where you are going to get there successfully. After finger tracing the design, you know your "road." As you stitch, keep your eyes ahead of the needle, just as in driving, so that you know what to expect and can compensate for it. This will immediately improve your workmanship and control. You will find that you will need to look ahead, look behind (in the rear view mirror), and look at where you are at, simultaneously. A lot like learning to drive, isn't it?

As you begin quilting, bring the bobbin thread up, hold onto both threads, and place the needle at the beginning of the line. Now, retrace the lines with your eyes so that you get used to the angle at which you are sitting and the light source. Lock off your stitching with very small stitches and cut the thread tails off. The secret to this is to not look at the needle or the hole inside the darning foot. Keep your eyes slightly ahead of the needle.

Remember your visualization experience. Quilt like you drive. Know where you are going before you get there. Your eyes will need to check on what you are doing, but only glance back and forth. Once you can do this, you will be able to stay on the line accurately and keep your stitches even. Let's work through some examples of this.

The stencil pattern in Figure 12.14 calls for a lot of loops to be quilted. When machine quilted, they all need to connect in the center. If you were to hand quilt this design, you would go through the layers to get from one loop to another. On the machine, this is not possible. You will need to stitch through the center three times. In order to hit the same spot each time, try putting a dot in the center of the design. As the loops are stitched, look at the dot before you get to it. Again, if you are looking at the needle or in the foot, you can only see where you are for a moment, and if the line curves, the momentum of your hands will take you past the curve before you can react and follow the line accurately. If you read the line ahead, you will be ready to go around the curve because you know where it is before you get to it.

FIG. 12.14 *Dot system for guidance*

Next is a design that is not continuous. Each brush stroke is separate from another. If these are quilted as drawn, you will need to stop and start at each design. Make them continuous by quilting the top half of each first, then finishing the bottom half last.

FIG. 12.15 *Making a design continuous*

To do this accurately, look ahead and plan for the stops and pattern. You will go over the top of the first pattern and continue on until the needle reaches the line of the second pattern. Right when the needle touches the second line, stop and stitch the tails. To do this, first visualize coming to a stop sign with your car. You do not wait until the white line is under the front tires to decide to stop. You look ahead of you about a half a block and see the white line. You plan the action needed to stop the car, and when you arrive at the white line, you have lifted your foot, applied the brake, and stopped the car exactly on the white line, without looking at it. Your eyes are still ahead of you assessing what needs to be done next. This same thought process will allow you to quilt this design. By looking at the second line before you get there, your hands will not know where else to go, so they will stop where your eye has stopped. Now stitch the tails and aim the needle back into the same needle hole that you made when you stopped for the line. Think of this as a dot, similar to the one in Fig. 12.14. Continue with the top sides of all the patterns.

FIG. 12.16 *Quilt top half first*

Now finish the bottom side, again looking ahead and finding the needle holes where you will need to stop in order to accurately close the design.

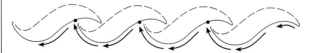

FIG. 12.17 *Finish with bottom half*

Points and corners always seem hard to the beginner, but there is an easy way to think through these. In order to create a point or a corner, you will need to allow the needle to stay in one place for just a heartbeat in order to make a couple of stitches. This creates the point or corner. **Note:** If you stay in the hole too long, the bobbin thread will tend to come up into the hole and cause an unsightly knot of thread.

To stitch straight lines straight, jump your eyes from one point to the next point, instead of following the line. If you are looking at where you need to be, your hands will take you there. If you follow the line with your eye, or look inside the darning foot, you will tend to wobble as you stitch.

FIG. 12.18 *Stop for a heartbeat at every dot*

When working with any quilt pattern, see what markings and helpers you can add to make it easier to stitch it accurately. It may be dots, arrows, or drawing the line solid instead of with the bridges the stencils give you.

If you are working with a design where you have to go from one area to another, do not cut the thread. Lock the threads, pull them across to the next area, lock them again at the beginning of the new line, and start stitching. After you finish with the design, clip all the extra threads.

Tip: If you find that you need to reposition your hands as you work through a design, stop with the needle in the down position. This will prevent the quilt from sliding and causing a loop of excess thread on the bottom of the quilt.

CONTINUOUS CURVE QUILTING

FIG. 12.19 *Continuous curve*

Continuous curve quilting is another form of free-motion quilting. I was introduced to this method several years ago by Barbara Johannah in her book, *Continuous Curve Quilting*. This method of quilting gives the look of hand-outline quilting without the starting, stopping and turning of the quilt under the needle to achieve traditional straight lines (Figure 12.19). Gentle arcs replace all of the straight lines and corners. The arcs go from corner to corner, with the deepest point 1/4" in from the seam at the center point of the line.

I took Barbara's idea one step further by using the darning foot. This eliminates the need for the turning that is necessary when working with a walking or regular foot. The darning foot allows you to go sideways, forward, and backward without turning and rotating. It also speeds up the process and allows all pieces in the block to be quilted.

CONTINUOUS CURVE EXERCISES

Plan your block strategy on graph paper. Start in an outside corner, trace through the block, and attempt to follow every side of every piece without stopping. Use gentle arcs from corner to corner. Other designs require you to start in the center of the block or along the side. See examples in Figures 12.20 and 12.21.

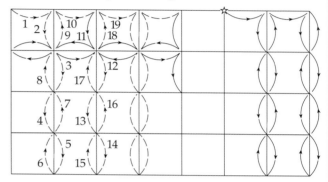

FIG. 12.20 *Continuous curve system—grid*

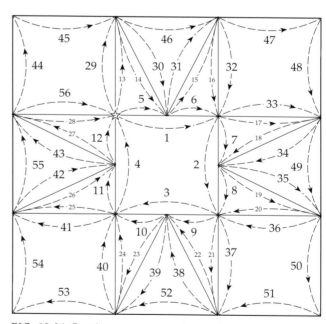

FIG. 12.21 *Continuous curve system—star*

If you follow the arrows in Figure 12.20 you can see how the line snakes from side to side to accommodate each side of each piece, instead of using short, jerky scalloped lines on the same side of each block. This procedure allows a fluid motion with your hands as you weave the line from side to side. Figure 12.21 starts inside the block and works out in a rotating manner.

In Figure 12.22, a long border of triangles is quilted by continually stitching only two sides of each triangle, then stitching back in a scallop motion to finish all of the third sides.

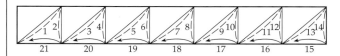

FIG. 12.22 *Continuous curve system — triangle border*

When you get comfortable with the feel of free-motion quilting, you will be able to "eyeball" the curves and just sew without marking. Until then, you may need to make a set of templates for these curves, and mark the lines on the quilt top to use as a guide. At the very least, mark a dot at the center point where the line goes into a piece the deepest (Figure 12.23). This dot system is similar to what we were doing with the previous patterns. If a dot is placed in the center of each seam, $1/4$" deep, your curves will likely be more accurate. Start with the needle in the corner, and look at the dot you are going to quilt toward. Start to quilt, and as you get near the dot, move your eye to the next corner. You will find a high rate of accuracy when you follow this procedure.

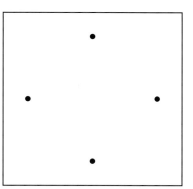

FIG. 12.23 $1/4$" *guide dots at center points*

To make the templates, draw a square, triangle, or whatever shape you are working with onto a piece of graph paper the finished size of the piece. Using a French curve or a flexible curve, connect two corners to make the arc. Be sure that the deepest part of the arc is in the center of the line and no more than $1/4$ inch deep.

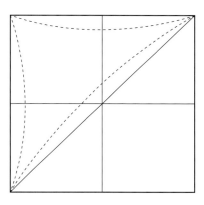

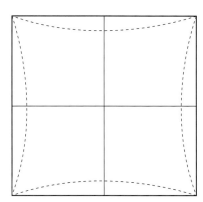

FIG. 12.24 *Continuous curve templates*

Make a complete set of templates for all the different sizes in the patchwork pieces. Use plastic to make a permanent set (Figure 12.24).

DITCH AND ECHO QUILTING

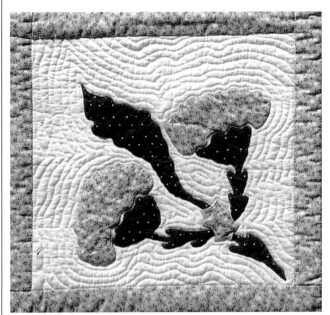

FIG. 12.25 Echo quilting

Ditch quilting around appliqués will allow the appliqué to stand up off the surface of the quilt and give you more texture. However, trying to ditch quilt with a walking foot around the intricate shapes is not practical or even possible. Instead, consider using the darning foot to move in and out of each shape.

When ditch quilting with a darning foot, you will need to look at the needle. This will let you know exactly where the needle is in relation to the edge of the appliqué. You will find that after all the training your eyes went through with the exercises, they will want to jump ahead and then look at the needle, then jump ahead again. If this is happening, you are getting control of free-motion quilting!

Echo quilting is the repeating of a shape as you move out from it; similar to the ripples created by dropping a pebble into a pool of water, the lines distort a little more as they go away from the design. Use this technique for appliqué designs, as well as silk-screened and stenciled fabrics, because it sets off the design well. Echo quilting can also be done by free-motion quilting with a darning foot. When first experimenting, you may want to lightly draw the quilting lines onto the fabric to get the feel of the design and to mark guidelines.

After awhile, you will find that doing it free-form under the needle is fun because you can see the interesting shapes develop as you stitch.

DITCH AND ECHO QUILTING EXERCISES

To begin, bury some tiny straight stitches in the ditch of your design or appliqué. The first quilting is done in the ditch around all edges of the design. Keep your eye on the needle. You do not want this stitching to show at all so the design will rise above the surface and have more puff. Ditch quilt every nook and cranny of the appliqué. The next line starts the echo process. Use the edge of your darning foot to measure the distance from the edge of the appliqué. This will make the line about $1/4$" outside the edge of the design. Work clockwise around the design, repeating every detail of the appliqué edge. As you come back to the beginning stitching, lock off the stitches again. Now move the foot out so that its edge is against the line you just completed. This will measure the next $1/4$" line out, and will expand the design.

Note: If possible, try to obtain a round darning foot for your machine, like the one pictured in Figure 12.1. This foot has $1/4$" on all sides of the needle, enabling me to measure off its edge regardless of which side is against the appliqué or stitching.

Continue this process until you are to the edge of the block. Eventually you will reach the outer edges and run off the fabric. Continue stitching into the corners until the entire block is "echoed." When you get to the outer seam, you can move to the next position by stitching in the ditch of the seam instead of locking off the thread. The seams become "highways" that allow you to get from one place to another without breaking the thread.

Printed panels, border prints, stenciled designs, and large prints can easily be quilted using this technique. The quilting can be as general as outlining the larger designs or as intricate as outlining every detail.

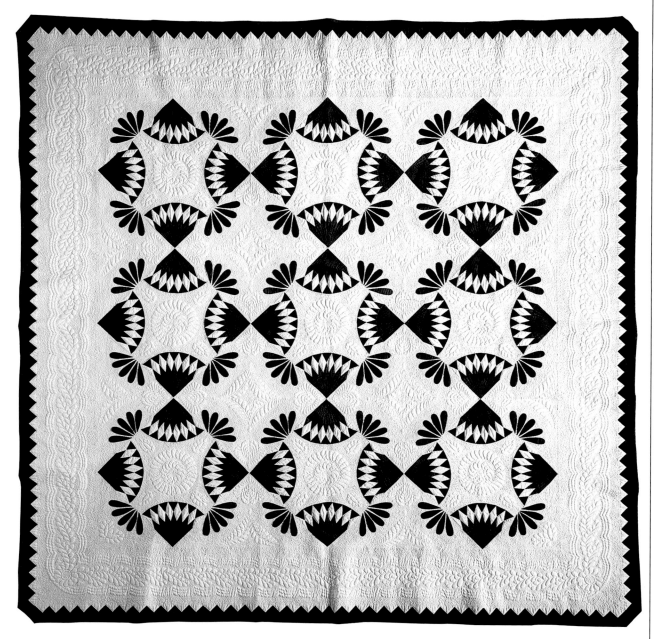

SPOON RIVER CHRISTMAS

*Machine pieced and quilted by Jean Lohmar, Galesburg, IL using free-motion and
stipple quilting techniques; cotton thread; Fairfield Cotton Classic® batting*
85" x 85"

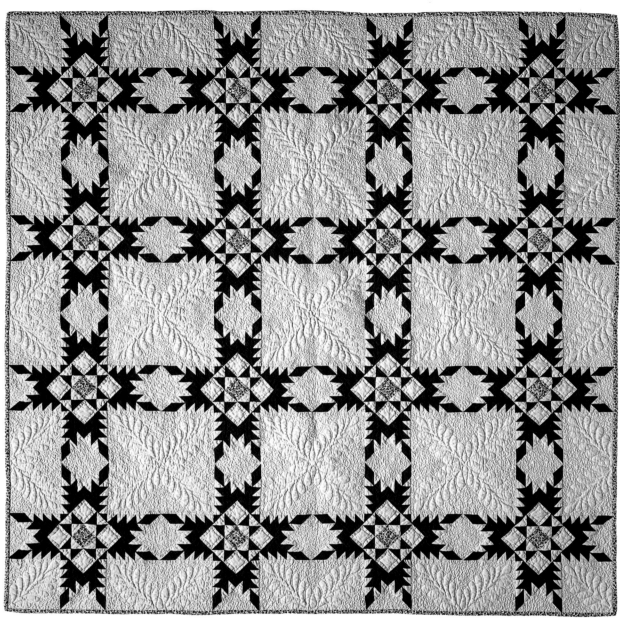

FEATHERED STAR

Machine pieced by Nancy Hieronymus Barrett, Edmond, OK; machine quilted by Harriet Hargrave using stipple, free motion, and continuous curve quilting techniques; DMC 50/2 cotton embroidery thread; Hobbs Heirloom® premium cotton batting 64" x 64"

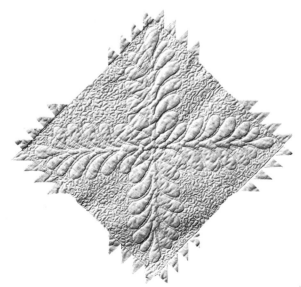

HEART OF HEARTS

1920's hand-appliquéd quilt; machine quilted using free-motion design quilting; cotton thread and batting; collection of Harriet Hargrave
72" x 85"

BALTIMORE GARDEN

Machine appliquéd by Barbara Trumbo;
machine appliquéd by Harriet Hargrave using
free-motion, ditch, grid, and line quilting
techniques; nylon thread; Mountain Mist®
Blue Ribbon 100% cotton batting
62" x 62"

PASTEL LOG CABIN

*1920's quilt top; machine quilted by
Harriet Hargrave using hanging diamond
grid quilting; nylon thread;
Hobbs Heirloom® premium cotton batting;
collection of Harriet Hargrave*
74" x 74"

STAR CHAIN

Machine pieced and quilted by Harriet Hargrave using continuous curve and free-motion quilting techniques; nylon thread; Mountain Mist® 100% natural batting
68" x 68"

CONFETTI BASKETS

*Adapted from a 1915 quilt made by Susan Anne Basbore Stouffer;
machine pieced and quilted by Harriet Hargrave using grid
and free-motion quilting techniques; nylon thread;
Mountain Mist® 100% natural cotton batting
59" x 59"*

LONE STAR

*Machine pieced and quilted by Sandy Espenschied, Atlanta,
GA using free-motion, continuous curve, and straight line
quilting techniques; nylon thread; Mountain Mist® 100%
natural cotton batting
80" x 90"*

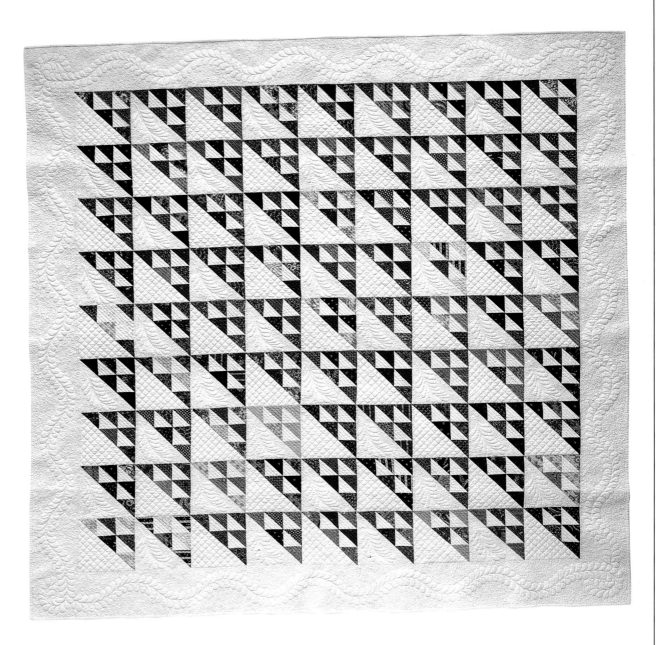

BIRDS IN THE AIR

*Machine pieced by JoAnn Morgan, Denver, CO; machine quilted by Harriet Hargrave
using free-motion, grid, and stipple quilting techniques; nylon thread;
Hobbs Heirloom® premium cotton batting
78" x 78"*

IDEAS FOR MACHINE QUILTING

STRAIGHT-LINE QUILTED QUILTS

PINEAPPLES AND LOG CABINS— HANGING DIAMOND GRID

Some quilts are not enhanced by ditch quilting. Often a quilt needs straight-line quilting, but stitching in the ditch alone will not add any surface texture. Log Cabins and many other quilts are so busy and complete in their design from the piecing or fabrics that fancy quilting is lost.

Therefore, an old, traditional way to achieve a heavy amount of quilting using straight lines—yet adding diagonal lines for interest— is stitching "hanging diamonds." This technique uses straight lines, parallel to the border, for the lengthwise direction of the quilt, then crosses the stitches with one-directional diagonal lines (Figures 13.1 and 13.2).

FIG. 13.1 Pineapple with hanging diamond quilting

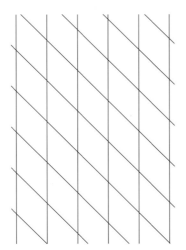

FIG. 13.2 *Hanging diamond grid*

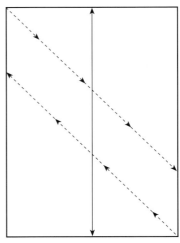

FIG. 13.4 *Diagonal anchoring—rectangular quilt*

When deciding which direction to quilt first, take into consideration the position of the lengthwise grain line of the backing fabric. Quilt with the lengthwise grain of the lining first, then quilt the crosswise or diagonal lines afterward. The quilt will remain square and much easier to control. This technique eliminates the drawing and stretching of the fabric between the stitching lines that occurs when working first with the bias, or stretchy crosswise grain.

Package the quilt for this example so that you can anchor the lengthwise center seam first. Next, anchor the diagonal direction so you will have anchor lines to cross as you quilt. If the quilt is square, this diagonal line will run from corner to corner (Figure 13.3).

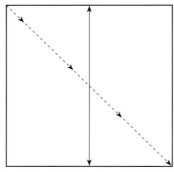

FIG. 13.3 *Diagonal anchoring—square quilt*

If the quilt is longer than it is wide, run two anchor lines diagonally, each one anchoring a different corner (Figure 13.4). Package the quilt so that you can quilt all lengthwise lines to the right of the center, top to bottom. Flip the quilt around, repackage, and quilt the seams from the right of the center, top to bottom. Now package the quilt diagonally, so that you are working from the center of the quilt out toward the corner. Flip the quilt around, and repackage so that you are repeating the process on the other half, working out to the corner. Throw these diagonal packages over your left shoulder to make them easier to work with.

Generally, this type of quilting extends into the border, so all that is left to do is trim, square, and bind. It gets easier all the time!

COMBINING DITCH AND FREE-MOTION QUILTING

The Amish Shadows quilt is a perfect example of combining techniques. The quilt is sewn together with straight set blocks, but each block has a diagonal seam.

Within one half of each block are four shorter seams. The opposite side is blank, leaving a space for a fancy design.

FIG. 13.5 Amish Shadows

FIG. 13.6 Block close-up

Start by quilting in the two anchor lines, one lengthwise and one crosswise. Continue with the system, until all straight lines are quilted.

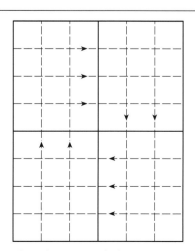

FIG. 13.7 Ditch quilting straight lines

Now repackage so that you can quilt the long, continuous diagonal lines that run through the center of each block. Work from the center to the right corner of each side.

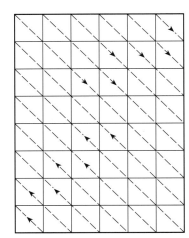

FIG. 13.8 *Ditch quilting diagonal lines*

Move on to the short, inner seams of each block. Use the darning foot and free-motion ditch quilt these lines. This eliminates the need to constantly move from one block to the next and lock and cut all the threads.

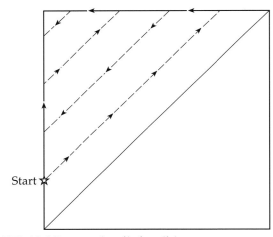

Start ☆

FIG. 13.9 *Free-motion ditch quilting*

With the darning foot, you can sew forward, backward, sideways, at angles, and in any direction you need to go, without turning the quilt or starting and stopping. The side ditches have already been quilted in the first process, but no harm is done by quilting them again. I use these ditches as highways to get from one place to another without breaking the thread.

It will take some practice to be able to put the needle where you want it all the time (on the low side), but perseverance will pay big dividends in speed and quality.

Star Chain, pictured on page 126, is another quilt that is a combination of ditch and free-motion quilting. Anytime a quilt can be ditch quilted without the stitching lines detracting from the desired surface texture, do it. This type of anchoring makes it easier to work with the larger areas in free-motion quilting. The layers are less likely to move and become distorted once they are stitched between the blocks.

On Star Chain, begin by anchoring the diagonal center seams. (Refer to page 91 for information on handling a diagonal set.) Stitch the first center diagonal seamline, repackage, and repeat for the opposite diagonal line. This will create an "X" through the center of the quilt. After anchoring, continue stitching each side from each anchor line, center to the right toward each corner. Repackage for each line.

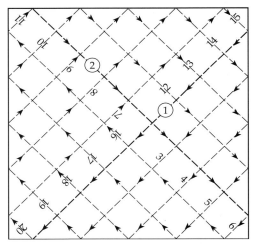

FIG. 13.10 *Anchoring and ditch quilting a diagonal set*

Once the ditch is stitched, repackage so that a "row" of blocks is exposed, and begin quilting down the row, one at a time, top to bottom. Complete all stitching that needs to be done within each block as you go. Once that row is completed, unroll the right side to expose the next row of blocks, fold up the left side, and repeat the process. Continue until all of the rows to the right are completed. Turn the quilt around, repackage, and repeat the process for the other side of the quilt. Quilt the borders and you are finished.

FREE-MOTION QUILTED QUILTS

FIG. 13.11 Double Irish Chain

DOUBLE IRISH CHAIN

Many quilts do not need ditch quilting. Straight lines may appear too harsh and stiff for the quilt's overall appearance. Ditch quilting might break into a secondary design developed by the patchwork, causing confusion when viewing the finished quilt. The Double Irish Chain baby quilt is an example of such a quilt top.

Ditch quilting between the blocks of this quilt would create a straight-line depression in what seems to be a diagonally appearing quilt. Long, straight diagonal lines through the double chain squares would appear too rigid and stiff. Therefore, ditch quilting is not appropriate for this top.

The design for this quilting pattern can be done totally with the darning foot in very little time. There is no need to use the anchoring system. Because the darning foot does not use the feed dogs, there is no pushing and pulling on the fabric from a feeding system. Use the same order for the quilting progress, but eliminate the first two steps for the anchoring lines.

Quilt this quilt block-by-block, row-by-row. Each block is completed as you go down the row. The Five-Patch pieced block, Block "A," is quilted with a zigzag pattern in a side-to-side movement. Either draw these lines onto the fabric, or eyeball them as you go.

FIG 13.12 Quilting illustration

Package the quilt so that the center row of blocks is exposed. Start with the first block in the row, the first row of the block. Position the needle into the fabric at the top left corner of the first square. Stitch toward the bottom right corner of that square, then continue up to the right top corner of the next square, the bottom right corner of the next, etc.

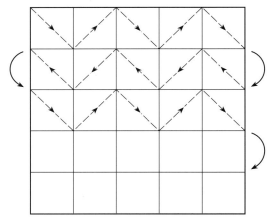

FIG. 13.13 Quilting system for Block "A"

Once that row is completed, lock off the stitches and pull the thread down to the next row. The needle will be placed in the first block on the right side of the second row. Do not cut the threads until you have locked off the stitches again. Lock off and start stitching to the left. With the needle in the lower right corner, stitch to the upper left corner of that square, down to the lower left corner of the next square, etc. Continue this process until all five rows are completed. **Note:** The corner squares of Block "B" will be combined with Block "A" when they align in the same rows.

Pull the thread into the center area of the connector Block "B," and quilt the design motif you have selected. Continue with the next Block "A." Once this row of blocks is completed, repackage the quilt for the next row of blocks to the right. Repeat the above process. When all rows to the right are finished, flip the quilt around so that the unquilted side is to your right. Repackage and repeat the process with this side. Quilt the borders last, then square and bind. You'll be amazed how fast you get the quilting finished when you use the darning foot.

NINE-PATCH AND HOURGLASS
The Nine-Patch and Hourglass (page 43) quilt presents a real challenge to machine quilting. Although there are a lot of straight lines, the use of a walking foot is not practical. Again, consider how many times you would need to start and stop or slightly turn the quilt. That makes the quilting difficult and time-consuming, and encourages distortion and puckering.

Each block is quilted separately as shown in Figures 13.14 and 13.15. Package the quilt to expose the center row of blocks. Quilt the four inner squares of the Nine-Patch block in a spiraling motion. Work from the outside edge in to the center of the square. Do not quilt the diagonal lines yet.

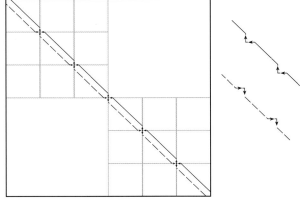

FIG. 13.14 Quilting lines for Nine-Patch

Next, move on to the connector block. Half of the block can be done at a time without breaking the thread. Begin in one corner of the triangle with straight lines. Work up and down the lines, using the ditches as highways, until you are at the opposite corner and all straight lines are finished (see Figure 13.15). Slip into the ditch and move into the dark triangle. Begin the inward spiral, locking off when you get to the innermost region. Pull the thread to the next light triangle and stitch with straight lines. Repeat the above process. This will allow you to quilt the entire connector block with only one thread break. Repeat for the four inner square spirals on the next block in the row, etc.

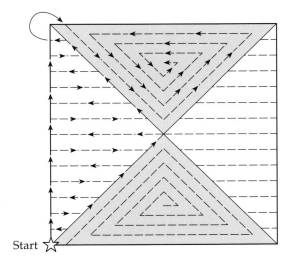

FIG. 13.15 Quilting lines for connecting block

Once this process has been completed for the entire quilt, you are ready to quilt the parallel diagonal lines through the Nine-Patches. Use the darning foot to eliminate turning the quilt

to accommodate the corners of the adjoining blocks. The ditches become "highways" again, to get from one square to the next, without stitching on top of the corner (see Figure 13.16).

FIG. 13.16 Continuous lines through Nine-Patch

Package the quilt for the diagonal lines (refer to page 91). Using the darning foot, quilt to the end of the line of the first square, glide into the ditch, and stitch in the ditch first one direction, then the other, then out again onto the diagonal line of the next square. Continue in this manner the distance of the total line, border to border. You can either quilt the parallel line next to the one just quilted backwards with the darning foot, or you can lock off the stitches and re-position the quilt to go forwards down the line.

The traditional fan pattern in the border is also simple to quilt with the darning foot. Each fan is done as a unit, following the line of the next to get from one row to another.

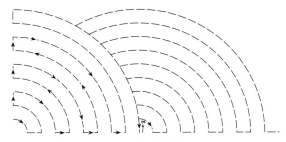

FIG. 13.17 Continuous stitched fans

This quilt can be quilted in approximately 14 hours using the darning foot. If you use a walking foot, you easily double the time investment and the stress level!

MEDALLION QUILTS

FIG. 13.18 Lone Star points quilted with continuous curve

LONE STAR

The Lone Star quilt pictured in the color section on page 127 is one of my favorites. Most quilters make a Lone Star at one time or another and it is usually ditch quilted. Ditch quilting is boring to do and boring to look at. I chose Barbara Johannah's continuous curve methods to quilt this quilt, and found it to be a delightful experience.

Medallions are more difficult to handle than straight and diagonal set quilts, and the system you have used up to now does not apply. Medallion quilts need to be quilted from the center out following the general dispersion of the pattern. Therefore, instead of a neat, tidy package, the quilt is opened up and free, making it easier to rotate the quilt to follow the circular pattern.

The Lone Star is made up of eight points. Each point shares a common pivot point, the center, where all eight points meet. Each point is made up of four to six rows, four to six diamonds to a row. One method for containing as much bulk as possible is to quilt each ring created by the points in a circular motion. But as you get out further into the star, you are moving a lot of fabric to follow the pattern.

Another method, which I prefer, breaks the star down into points, and you work one point at a time. Package the quilt as neatly as possible. You will find that it needs to be opened up quite a bit to accommodate the size of the star point. The package will be messy and more awkward than with previous quilts. Start with the center pivot point. Move to the right, into the first row of the first point. Stitch a continuous curve line from the pivot point to the top right corner, stitch down the right side of the first diamond, back up the first side of the second diamond, across the top of the second, down the right side, up the left side of the third diamond, across the top and down the right side, etc. (Figure 13.19).

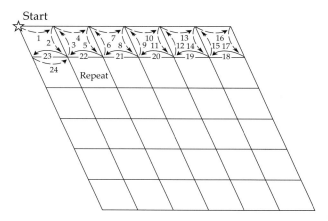

FIG. 13.19 Continuous curve system

Once you are at the end of row one, come back toward the center pivot point, stitching the curved line along the bottom side of each diamond on the first row. Do not go back up to the pivot point; instead, repeat this process for the second row of diamonds.

Continue this process until all rows of the first point are finished. Come back to the pivot point by stitching the curved lines up the side of the point, into the pivot point (Figure 13.20). Now you are ready to rotate the entire quilt until the first row of the second point is lined up to your right. Repeat as you did for point one.

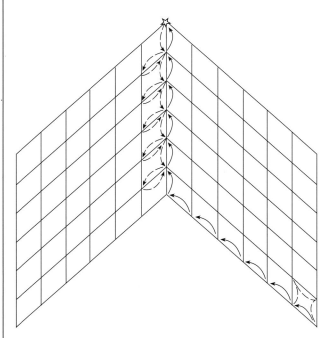

FIG. 13.20 Starting second point

This process eliminates the need to constantly lock off and cut threads. The only time this is necessary is when you run out of bobbin thread.

OHIO ROSE

The Ohio Rose quilt pictured on page 104 is a good example of echo quilting. To begin, package the quilt so that the center row of appliqué blocks is exposed. Start quilting in the ditch around the appliqué, free-motion with a darning foot. You will need to guide the block so that the needle runs along the edge of each appliqué piece. This is also a good time to do the inside surface quilting of each petal and leaf. With a small amount of double-stitching in certain ditches, this can all be done in one continuous motion.

FIG. 13.21 Ditch and outline quilting

Proceed to the echo quilting. Let the edge of the darning foot ride along the ridge of the appliqué pieces. This will measure the distance consistently around the entire appliqué. Continue around the appliqué until you meet the point where you started. This should give you a quilting line approximately 1/4" from the edge of the appliqué around the block. Repeat this procedure allowing the edge of the darning foot to follow the quilting line that you just finished. Continue doing this until the echo lines reach the seamline of the block. Go to the next block and repeat. Repeat the process until all appliqué blocks are quilted to their seamlines.

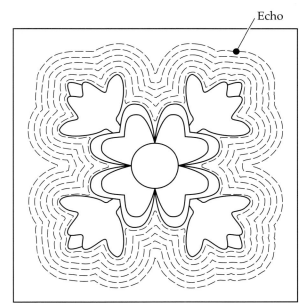

Echo

FIG. 13.22 Echo quilting

Once each block is echoed to the seamline, you will see that there are "puddles" left between each block (Figure 13.23). Quilt these areas by working from the previously quilted lines, working in to the center of each puddle. Each round of quilting will be separate, not continuous. Remember to lock the stitches well at the beginning and end of every line.

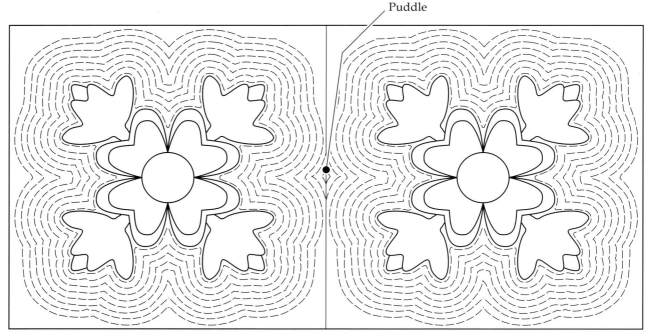

Puddle

FIG. 13.23 *Echo quilting puddle*

Once all the blocks are quilted, you are ready
to move into the border. Crosshatch quilting
is very effective on this quilt. The border
layers may shift or become distorted if great
care is not taken. Approach the border from
the centers out. Start at the border seamline
and stitch out toward the raw edge. Stitch all
lines of the same direction first, starting in the
center of the border and progressing to the
corner. Repeat this for the other half of the
border. Once the entire border is quilted once,
repeat the process and do the crossing lines.
Use your hands, and be careful that the fabric
does not "draw" between the quilting lines;
it should lie flat and smooth.

The quilts shown here exemplify the various
approaches to machine quilting. Every quilt
will be slightly different, but general rules
always seem to apply to help you create a
beautiful quilt by machine.

By now, all this information should affect
your way of thinking. Look at your collection
of quilts and quilt tops, and imagine how you
might machine quilt each project.

❖ PART FOUR ❖
FINISHING
UP

BINDING

Once the quilt is completely quilted, you are ready to trim the edges, square the corners, and apply the binding. Binding causes most quilters to groan, but once you know the tricks that make it easy, it no longer seems such a dreadful task.

After you complete the quilting, clip all stray threads and check for any missed quilting lines or loose stitches. Trim the edges and square the corners into perfect 90° angles.

HALF-INCH BINDING

If you want to finish your quilt with a standard $1/2$" binding, trim the quilt so that you have a little less than $1/4$" of batting and lining beyond the edge of the top. This fills the width of the binding that extends beyond the seam allowance. When wrapping the binding around the edge, be sure the binding is filled to the edge with the quilt to prevent excess wear on the folded edge.

For reproduction quilts, you will want to consider a narrower binding. I like to use a $3/8$" binding. I find that trimming the batting and lining even with the quilt top is sufficient to fill this narrow of a binding.

Straight-grain binding is preferred over bias binding when binding a straight-edge quilt; it keeps the quilt edge straight with no ripples. A bias binding is "stretchy" and may give the quilt a stretched appearance along the edge. The quilt appears to ripple when hung or placed on a bed. Use bias binding only when a quilt has rounded corners or scallops.

Note: The argument for bias is that the edge does not wear as badly because there is not a single thread in the weave that runs along the edge (as in straight-grain binding).

My argument here is that when I cut my crosswise strips to make the binding, I fold the selvages to the folded edge, and 99% of the time, the grain is off on the bolt. Therefore, the strips are not perfectly on grain, yet they are not true bias. This gives me the best of both methods, since the grain is slightly off, allowing more threads to take the wear, but it is not nearly as stretchy as bias.

Cut the binding strips $2^1/2$" wide for $1/2$" finished binding and 2" wide for $3/8$" binding. You can use the lengthwise or crosswise grain. Crosswise grain has a slight amount of stretch, so be careful not to stretch it when applying it to the edge of the quilt. Do not mix strips cut from both grains. The color will appear to be different, and the fabric will behave differently.

Measure the outer edge of the quilt to find the total length of binding required. Add 12 inches to this measurement. You will need about $2/3$ yard of fabric to produce the 30 feet of binding needed to go around a 80" x 90" quilt. Cut nine strips of fabric, each measuring $2^1/2$" wide by 45" long (if using the crosswise width). Cut each end of the strip at a 45° angle (bias) following Figure 14.1. Join these strips using a bias seam (Figure 14.2).

FIG. 14.1 Cut binding strip

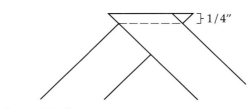

FIG. 14.2 Binding

Keep joining the strips with the right sides together until you have a continuous piece of binding (Figure 14.3). Strips are joined together in this way so the layers from the seams won't stack up and leave a lump as they are applied to the quilt. Instead, the seams will spiral to distribute the bulk evenly.

FIG. 14.3 *Joining strip ends*

Press the seams open. Fold the 2¹/₂"-wide strip in half, lengthwise, making a strip 1¹/₄" wide. Starting in the center of one side of the quilt, lay the raw edges of the binding on the raw edge of the quilt top. Begin sewing, leaving about 8" of the strip free behind the foot for joining later. Stitch ¹/₄" from the raw edge down the length of the quilt. When approaching a corner, stop ¹/₄" from the edge.

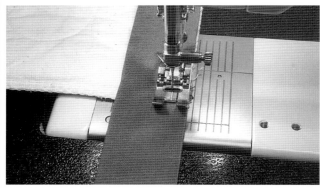

FIG. 14.4 *Stop ¹/₄" from ends*

Tip: Check to see if the bar in front of your needle on the presser foot measures ¹/₄". Many do, and this is an excellent way to know when to stop.

Leaving the needle in the fabric, turn the quilt 90° so you are ready to stitch down the next edge. Instead of sewing forward, backstitch off the edge.

FIG. 14.5 *Backstitch off edge*

Fold the binding straight up, away from the corner, to form a 45° angle fold (Figure 14.6).

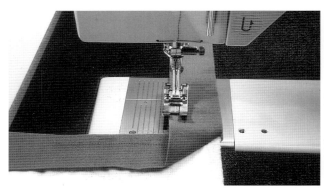

FIG. 14.6 *First fold for miter*

Bring the binding straight down in line with the next side to be sewn (Figure 14.7). The fold must rest along the top edge of the quilt, and the two folded edges on the left should be exactly aligned. Do not skimp on this fold or the miter will not be accurate. Begin stitching the next side at the top of the fold, stitching through all thicknesses. Miter each corner in this manner.

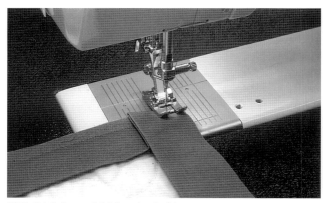

FIG. 14.7 *Second fold and stitching on top*

As you approach the starting point, stop about 16" from the beginning stitches. This allows plenty of room to join the ends on the bias. Overlap the loose ends of binding where they meet. Lay the ends of the Side 2 binding strip flat, and lay the beginning end of Side 1 on top of Side 2, keeping both binding strips folded. Label the long point of Side 1 "A." Label the short point of Side 1 "B."

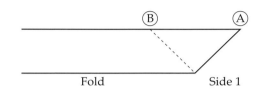

FIG. 14.8 Labeling side one

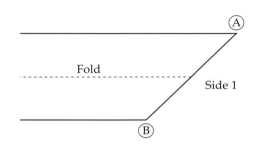

FIG. 14.9 Labeling side one

Mark dot A onto the top layer of Side 2. Mark dot B onto the bottom layer of Side 2.

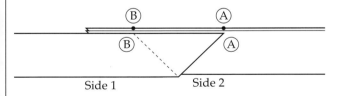

FIG. 14.10 Marking side two

Open Side 2 and measure ¹/₂" to the left of these dots. This provides seam allowances. Cut on this line.

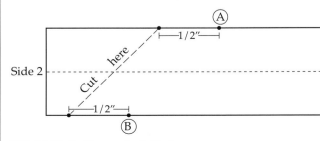

FIG. 14.11 Cutting end of side two

Open Side 1. With right sides together, stitch Side 1 to Side 2 using a ¹/₄" seam allowance.

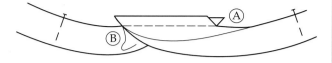

FIG. 14.12 Stitching ends together

Press the seam open. Fold the joined strip in half and press. The binding should be a perfect fit. Finish stitching the binding to the edge of the quilt.

Wrap the binding over the raw edge to the back of the quilt. Fold the edge under, and place the folded edge of the binding on top of the stitching line. Sew a very tiny blindstitch to secure the binding. A blindstitch should be no longer than ¹/₄" and should not show on the front or back. If properly stitched, the blindstitch gives an almost invisible finish. Slide the needle through the folded edge and at the same point, pick up one or two threads of the lining fabric. Continue doing this, taking stitches ¹/₈" to ¹/₄" apart. Space the stitches evenly.

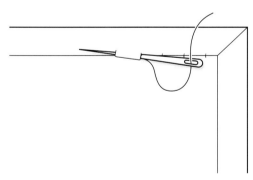

FIG. 14.13 Finishing the edge

A perfect miter at the corner is already formed on the top of the quilt. On the back, form a miter and continue to secure with blindstitching. The fold of this miter should be the opposite direction from the one on the right side, so the bulk of the miter will be evenly distributed.

FIG. 14.14 *Finished corner—front side*

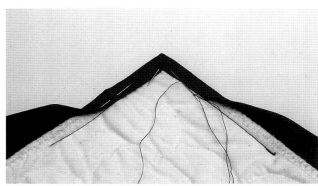

FIG. 14.15 *Back side—blindstitching*

Below is an estimate of the yardage needed to bind various size quilts with straight-grain binding. These measurements are based on $1/2$" finished binding.

Wallhanging 36" x 36"	5 strips x 2^1/$_2$" wide = 12.5" = ^{3}/$_8$ yard.
Twin 54" x 90"	8 strips x 2^1/$_2$" wide = 20" = ^{5}/$_8$ yard.
Double 72" x 90"	8 strips x 2^1/$_2$" wide = 20" = ^{5}/$_8$ yard.
Queen 90" x 108"	10 strips x 2^1/$_2$" wide = 25" = ^{3}/$_4$ yard.
King 120" x 120"	12 strips x 2^1/$_2$" wide = 30" = ^{7}/$_8$ yard.

If you choose to make bias binding, the easiest way is to use the continuous method. The chart on page 145 will help you determine how big to cut your square based on the amount of binding needed.

Step 1: Cut a square of fabric the size needed. Cut the square in half diagonally, creating two triangles.

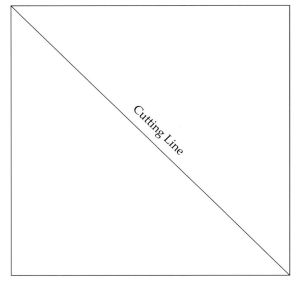

FIG. 14.16 *Cutting square in half diagonally*

Step 2: Sew these triangles together as shown in Figure 14.17 with a $1/4$" seam allowance.

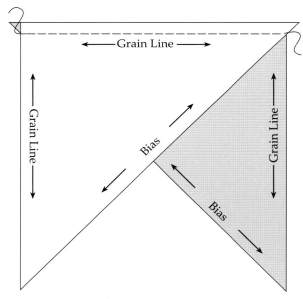

FIG. 14.17 *Sewing the two triangles together*

Step 3: After sewing, open the triangles and press the seam open. This will give you a parallelogram. Using a ruler, mark the entire back side with lines spaced the width you need to cut your bias. Cut on the first line about 5".

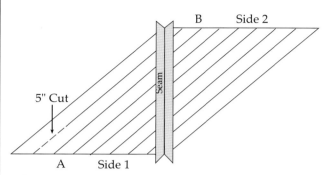

FIG. 14.18 *Press seam open, measure and draw lines*

Step 4: Connect A and B and side 1 and side 2 to form a tube. (The cut edge on the first line will line up with the raw edge at B. This will allow the first line to be offset by one line). Pin the raw ends together, making sure that the lines match. Sew with a ¼" seam allowance.

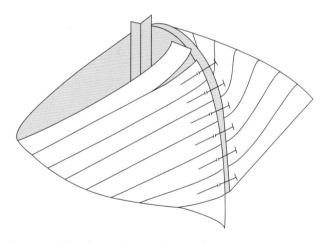

FIG. 14.19 *Offset by one line and sew tube*

If you have aligned the seam properly, you will have an extra strip at each end. Continue cutting on the line you started in Step 3. As you cut on the line, the tube will become one long piece of bias.

Here is an easy formula for figuring the size of square you need for the required length of bias: Divide the square size by the width of your bias, then multiply only the whole number of the answer by the square size again. Example: a 22" square divided by 2¹/₂" (width of bias) = 8.80. Multiply 8 by 22 = 176" of bias yielded. If you need this in yardage, divide by 36.

	Bias needed
Wallhanging 36" x 36" ÷ 156"	(4¹/₂ yards) = 22" square
Twin 54" x 90" ÷ 300"	(8¹/₂ yards) = 28" square
Double 72" x 90" ÷ 336"	(9¹/₂ yards) = 30" square
Queen 90" x 108" ÷ 408"	(11¹/₂ yards) = 33" square
King 120" x 120" ÷ 492"	(14¹/₂ yards) = 38" square

ONE-INCH BORDER BINDING

The 1"-wide border binding is fun and fast. The wide-finished binding also serves as a small border or frame for the quilt.

Cut strips $5^1/2$" wide. If you need additional length to make the border for one side of the quilt, join the strips on the bias as described under $1/2$" binding (Figures 14.1 and 14.2). Do not join all the strips together this time as you did for $1/2$" binding. The strips should be 5" to 6" longer than each side of the quilt. Fold the strips in half lengthwise, making them $2^3/4$" wide, and press.

To prepare the quilt top, trim the backing and batting to $3/4$" beyond the edge of the quilt top. The remainder will be enclosed within the binding. Sew the binding onto one side of the quilt top, starting and stopping $1/4$" from the raw edge (the seam line) that is perpendicular to the edge you are sewing (Figure 14.20).

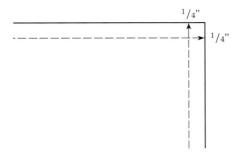

FIG. 14.20 Sew 1/4 inch from raw edges

A $2^1/2$" to 3"-wide tail of binding has been left at each end of each border strip. Now join these tails at the corners to make perfect miters by folding one edge's tail back so that it lies perfectly on the binding (see arrow in Figure 14.21). Lay the other side over it. Draw a line on the top piece that extends the seam line of the binding piece that is on the bottom. This line is AB.

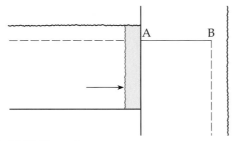

FIG. 14.21 Preparing corner

Find the measurement that is halfway between the folded edge and the seam line of AB. C is the midpoint of line AB. Draw a line from C that is at a right angle to AB (perpendicular). On this line, measure up from C the same distance as AC or CB. This point is D. *Example: If AC = $1^1/4$ inches then CB should = $1^1/4$ inches and CD should = $1^1/4$ inches.*

Draw in a sewing line that goes from A to D and D to B.

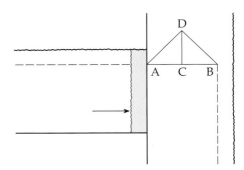

FIG. 14.22 Developing sewing line

Open both sides of the binding and fold the quilt diagonally from the corner. Align both binding strips so that their edges are exactly even and their corners match. Pin in place and sew line ADB. Backstitch at the beginning and end. At the point, you might need to take a stitch across the point to keep it perfect. Stop stitching one stitch from the point, take one stitch across to the other side, and continue down line DB (see Figures 14.23, 14.24, and 14.25).

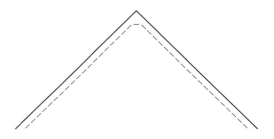

FIG. 14.23 One stitch across triangle tip

FIG. 14.24 Marking triangle

FIG. 14.25 Stitched and trimmed

Use a point turner to straighten the point and roll the binding to the back. The folded edge should align with the seam line on the back, making a perfect mitered corner on the front and back. Stitch in place by hand or machine.

FIG. 14.26 Finished corner

Binding can be finished working from the top by ditch-stitching with a machine using matching or nylon thread. Roll the binding to the back, with the fold just slightly beyond the stitching line. With the pin heads toward you, pin the binding in the ditch on the top side of the quilt. To stitch in place, guide the machine needle exactly in the ditch, removing the pins as you come to them. No stitching should show on the top, and the binding edge should just be caught by the stitches on the back (Figure 14.27). If finishing by hand, use a blindstitch.

FIG. 14.27 Finishing by ditch stitching

CARE AND KEEPING

ow that your work is finished, proper care and storage of your quilt will ensure years of joy, beauty, and pride. A machine-pieced and quilted quilt is not as fragile as one pieced and quilted by hand. It will probably be used more, but we make quilts to use, enjoy, and share.

LAUNDERING YOUR QUILTS

GUIDELINES FOR THE CARE OF COTTON AND POLYESTER QUILTS

There seems to be a lot of anxiety about caring for quilts, whether they are new or antique! Quilters overlook the fact that the soil trapped in the fibers can often cause more damage than the actual laundering process. Textiles are more sensitive to light, airborne dust, pollution, and stains than most other art objects. Consider what the fabric has been exposed to during construction: body oil from your hands, lint from being handled, soil from being on the floor a few times. No wonder the quilt is usually quite soiled upon finishing.

Start the cleaning process by vacuuming. This will remove dust particles whose sharp edges start to cut away at the fibers. Buy a 2'-square piece of fiberglass screening and bind the edges with twill tape. Place the screen on the quilt. Using the corner attachment of the vacuum, gently vacuum over the screen, cleaning the front and the back of the quilt.

A bath is needed to remove dirt and stains, but washing can permanently damage the quilt if care is not taken. Test for colorfastness in today's cottons whether you prewash your new fabrics or not. Many quilts have bled when they were washed the first time, even though the fabrics were prewashed. This staining is often irreversible. With care, the fabrics used in the quilt can look as fresh and new after the first laundering as they did originally.

Choose a safe washing agent for cleaning your quilts. A rule of thumb when selecting a product is to find something you would be willing to take a bath in. This automatically eliminates general laundry detergents which can cause bleeding, fading, and rapid aging of cotton fabrics. Highly recommended products are Orvus Paste®, Ivory Clear Dishwashing Soap®, and Mountain Mist Ensure®. Orvus Paste is recommended overall because it is a neutral product that rinses out of the quilt thoroughly. It is also packaged under various names and available at quilt shops.

FIG. 15.1 *Care products*

Color testing should be done for every fabric in the quilt, not just the ones you might think could bleed. (Remember, if the quilt bleeds in washing, it could be irreversible, and prewashing should not be relied on solely for colorfastness.) If you have seven different blues in the quilt, test all seven. Start by rubbing a dry, white cloth gently over each fabric to see if any color rubs off. If not, dampen the cloth with cool tap water and rub it over the fabric. If no color appears, the next step is to use warm water, and if that is safe, use warm water with the diluted washing agent you have chosen. I generally mix 1 teaspoon Orvus® to 1 quart of warm water.

If any of the fabrics bleed, do not wash the quilt. I have had experiences where the detergent was not safe, and bleeding occurred. Treat any bleeding immediately because the damage can be permanent if the quilt is allowed to dry. I have had excellent results with Easy Wash®, a soil and stain remover for natural fibers. Fill the washer with cold water and add ³/₄ to 1 cup of Easy Wash concentrate. Soak the quilt in this solution for 15 minutes. (Easy Wash can be applied directly to stained areas as well.) Rinse and check for fading. If the color is gone, proceed to drying. If the color is still apparent, repeat the process. Snowy Bleach® is another product that removes excess color when bleeding has occurred. These products are by no means guaranteed to solve the problem, but they do have a good track record.

If the color tests show that the fabrics do not bleed, you can proceed with the washing. (We are discussing the care of new quilts here, not antiques. Consult a textile conservator concerning the care of antique quilts of value.)

I launder my quilts in the washing machine. Fill the washer to its largest capacity with warm water. A rule of thumb is to use the temperature you use to bathe a baby. Add the Orvus or your chosen washing agent and agitate to dissolve. Turn the washer off and gently add the quilt. Completely immerse the quilt and let it soak for ten minutes. Then gently move the quilt in the water with your hands to release the soil from the fabric.

Do this for about five minutes. Detergent has the ability to clean for only 12 to 15 minutes. If the water is very soiled, you will need to repeat this process until the quilt appears clean. (Soaking in the same water for a long period of time will not get the quilt clean.)

Spin the water out of the quilt on the gentle spin cycle. Spinning will not harm the quilt, and is much easier on the fibers than handling a heavy, dripping-wet quilt. **Note:** This method is not recommended for king-size quilts. Extra large, front-loading washers are recommended for laundering any large spread or quilt.

To rinse, carefully remove the quilt from the washer and fill the tub with warm water. Keep the water temperature for washing and rinsing the same. Place the quilt in the water and gently move it around to remove the washing agent from the fibers. Drain the water and spin. If possible, watch as the water drains from the tube. If soapy residue continues to come from the water, rinse again. The water should run completely clear at the end of the cycle to indicate that the quilt is thoroughly rinsed. This may take as many as five rinsings, depending on the washing agent and amount of detergent used.

There are differing opinions on how to dry a quilt, but do not put a wet quilt in the clothes dryer! The tumbling action is hard on the quilt. It can also cause crocking (the surface loss of color by friction) and streaking of the fabric colors. I think the best way to dry a quilt is to lay it flat. I prefer to dry quilts outdoors on a dry, breezy, sunny day. I use two sheets— one on the ground and one on top of the quilt—to protect the quilt from insects and the sun. Grommets can be put in the corners of the sheets so they can be staked down to prevent blowing in the breeze. When the top is dry to the touch, turn it over to dry the bottom. I have also had success drying quilts over large bushes. Cover the bush with a sheet, lay the quilt over the bush, and cover with another sheet. The bush allows the quilt to be off the ground, yet provides total support and air circulation.

If you need to dry indoors, lay the quilt on the floor, using sheeting or plastic to protect the floor. Oscillating fans will speed the drying process considerably. Creating a large drying screen from a piece of mosquito netting, fiberglass screen, etc., can also be helpful in getting the quilt off the floor and aiding air circulation. Never hang a wet quilt because the pressure of hanging can weaken the fabrics and tear the stitches. When the quilt is barely damp dry, you can fluff the quilt a bit by placing it in the dryer on air or fluff—no heat.

Remember to use the most natural ways to wash and store your treasured quilts. Go back and think about the old ways of doing things. Our grandmothers had more common sense than we seem to have. Our harsh chemicals and push-button machines have caused many things to be ruined.

GUIDELINES FOR THE CARE OF WOOL QUILTS

Today's wool battings are made to be washable without undue shrinkage. With proper care, quilts with wool batting will endure much longer than those with polyester.

Wash wool quilts in cool to lukewarm water (about 85° F). A cold water wash and rinse is best for the wool, but if the quilt is soiled, warm water will assist the cleaning process. It is very important to keep the wash and rinse water temperatures as close to one another as possible.

The ideal way to wash a wool quilt is by hand. Agitation should be minimal, if done at all, and only on the gentle cycle. Wash for 30–45 seconds, then let the quilt soak for 4–5 minutes, followed by about 1 minute of light agitation. Rinse by gently agitating for 30–45 seconds then spin the water out. Repeat if necessary. The more agitation the quilt is put through, the more shrinkage is likely to occur. Spinning does not damage the wool in any way, so it is preferable to spin on gentle to remove excess water after washing and rinsing. This also reduces drying time.

If at all possible, lay the quilt flat to dry. The dryer causes excessive agitation, and the uneven heat causes shrinkage. If you must dry in the dryer, do it on the lowest heat setting. If possible, dry the quilt flat until just damp, then tumble for a few minutes to fluff and soften the fabric.

Be very careful when choosing a washing agent for wool quilts. An alkaline detergent can cause wool fibers to shrink even in cool water. You will want to use a neutral, non-ionic detergent that does not contain enzymes, fabric brighteners, or whiteners. Orvus Paste® is a perfect choice for wool quilts, as well as any detergents recommended by the American Wool Council.

Keep your wool quilts clean. Heavy soiling is not only hard on the fabrics, but excessive washing to remove heavy soiling is harder on the wool than more frequent launderings.

Finally, the more the wool is quilted, the more the quilt is stabilized and the chance of any shrinkage is lessened.

STORING QUILTS IN THE HOME

When not in use, quilts should be stored carefully. We tend to think that only old or antique quilts need special care and consideration. However, if new quilts are to remain beautiful and damage-free in the years to come, you need to consider how they are cared for today. Quilts are ideally stored unfolded, flat, and unstacked. However, few of us have the luxury of this kind of space.

Avoid storing quilts, or any textiles, in attics or basements. Attics are too hot and basements are too damp. Ideal storage temperatures are between 60° and 70° F. Humidity levels need to be between 45% and 60%. Humidity is the real killer for quilts—they cause mold and mildew problems. Quilts should be stored within the living area of your home, preferably away from outside walls, and in an area with air circulation that is dark most of the time. A good guideline is that if the temperature and humidity level are comfortable to you, it will also be good for your quilts.

Avoid using plastic bags. Plastic cuts off air circulation and emits harmful by-products as it ages. The static electricity generated by plastics attracts dust, which is also undesirable. Finally, mold and mildew result from moisture trapped inside plastic bags. If you see little black spots on a quilt, which indicate mildew, very little can be done. (Mildew can also be detected by the odor.) Prevent mildew with good air circulation.

Use well-washed cotton muslin sheeting or acid-free tissue paper to protect quilts from wood surfaces, dust, light, and abrasion. Fabric wrappings can be washed once a year; tissue paper needs to be changed at least that often.

FOLDED STORAGE

Storing a folded quilt presents a major problem: Fold lines create stress on the quilted fabric, stitches, and batting. You can reduce this stress by padding the folded areas with tissue paper or cotton sheeting. Lay the quilt out on a clean, flat surface. Place a sheet of acid-free tissue paper on the center of the quilt.

Make a crumpled roll and place it across the quilt so that the top $1/3$ of the quilt can be folded over the roll. Place another roll of paper across the lower $1/3$ of the quilt, and fold the lower third over the roll. Now the quilt is folded in thirds. Place a shorter roll of paper across the folded quilt $1/3$ of the way in. Fold the left side toward the center. Repeat with the right side. Avoid stacking quilts if possible, as this counteracts the tissue paper padding (see Figures 15.2 through 15.10).

Once the quilt has been folded, it is ready for storage. Acid-free boxes are a good choice if your space is limited and you need to stack the quilts. A box reduces stress on the quilt directly, but it also reduces air circulation.

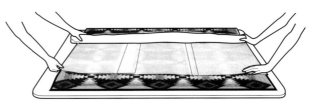

FIG. 15.2 *Tissue roll for top third of quilt*

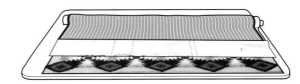

FIG. 15.3 *Top third folded over roll*

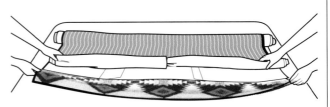

FIG. 15.4 *Tissue roll for bottom third*

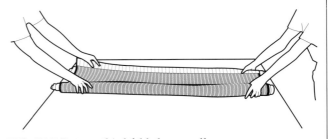

FIG. 15.5 *Bottom third folded over roll*

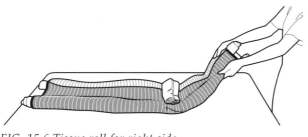

FIG. 15.6 Tissue roll for right side

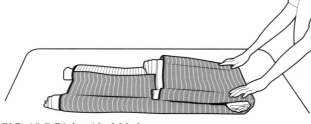

FIG. 15.7 Right side folded

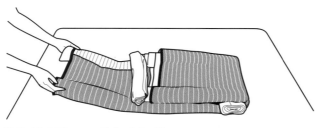

FIG. 15.8 Tissue roll for left side

FIG. 15.9 Left side folded

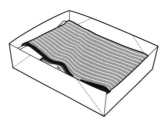

FIG. 15.10 Stored in acid-free box

If you store your quilts in a blanket chest or cedar chest, be very careful that the fabric does not come into direct contact with the wood, especially if the wood is unsealed like cedar. Wood gives off detrimental acids, so you will need several layers of protective material between the wood and fabric. Wrap your quilt in well-washed cotton sheeting before storing near a wood surface. If the quilt will be on a shelf, put several coats of polyurethane on the wood before placing the quilt on it. Even then, line the shelves with acid-free tissue paper.

Refold the quilts frequently, and avoid folding on a previous crease, on a tear, or on any other wear mark. Fold a different direction each time, whether in halves, thirds, or in triangles like a flag.

ROLLED STORAGE

There is some controversy as to whether or not a quilt should be rolled. Some conservators say that only single-layer textiles should be rolled, while others say that quilts can benefit from this technique. If you have the space, your quilts can be rolled around a large tube measuring at least 3" in diameter. It should be longer than the width of the quilt. Cover the tube with cotton fabric or tissue paper. (The cover will need to be renewed once a year.) Roll the quilt loosely, avoiding wrinkles, with the top to the inside if it is a pieced quilt. This puts minimum stress on the stitches. Once the quilt is rolled, cover it with a clean cotton sheet. The tubes, if strong enough, can be stored on wall brackets in a dark, clean, well-ventilated area. If the tube is too weak, run a strong rod through it (Figures 15.11 and 15.12).

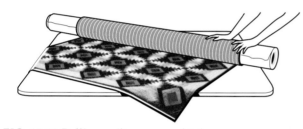

FIG. 15.11 Rolling quilt on covered tube

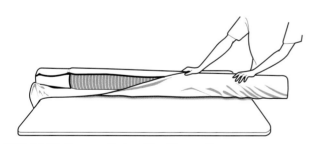

FIG. 15.12 Cover rolled quilt with muslin

All quilts need to spend some time opened out and on their backs. It is suggested by quilt curators to air them every six months or at least once a year. Lay them on the floor or on a bed for several days. On a dry, warm day, lay them on the grass to air for three or four hours. This will give you a chance to wash their coverings to remove dust and wood acids that may have been absorbed.

Once a quilt is stored, don't forget about it for long periods of time. Even with careful storage, pests can cause problems. At least once a year, the quilt needs to be refolded and have its wrapping washed or replaced. While doing this, carefully vacuum the quilt surfaces to remove moth eggs, dust particles, etc. Moth crystals in the vacuum bag will kill any insects sucked up in the cleaning process so they can't escape.

If you have problems with moths in wool or wool-filled quilts, there are several solutions. One is to dry-clean the item. You can also try freezing the quilt for about two months, or vacuuming then treating with moth balls (paradichlorobenzene, PDCB). Do not use Naphthalene® moth balls. One method given by Michael Kile of The Quilt Digest Press, is to use two garbage bags, one inside the other. Loosely fold the quilt and place it in the bags. Put a lot of PDCB moth balls in a cotton cloth, then twist and tie at the top. Make sure this bag of moth balls sits on top of the quilt. Tightly seal the bag and leave it for at least a week, possibly two. The warmer the temperature (preferably around 70°), the better this treatment works. Mothballs are a good general treatment for all insects.

If you need to treat an area for insects, suspend a cloth bag full of moth balls from the ceiling in your storage closet. The fumes are heavier than air, so the bag needs to be placed above the items you want to treat. Use a heavy concentration of PDCB for two months, rather than a small amount continuously. Do not allow the chemical to come into direct contact with the fabrics.

Avoid having your best quilts around smokers. Cigarette smoke soaks into fabric faster and deeper than anything. Smoke can cause color changes and it also speeds the deterioration of the fibers in the quilt.

Because quilts are an art form and are valuable not only in dollars, but in sentimental attachment, they deserve special attention. A new quilt, as well as one made many years ago, can be ruined by improper storage, display, use, and cleaning. Treat quilts with care, and they will bring you joy for many, many years.

HANGING AND DISPLAYING YOUR QUILTS

Quilts are generally made as functional showpieces and are of little value if stored away and not seen and enjoyed. However, care needs to be taken if the quilt is to be hung for display. Quilts on display should be rotated, so that one quilt does not hang for long periods of time. It is hard to notice changes occurring in the textiles when we see them constantly. Continued exposure is bad for the fibers and dyes of the fabrics in quilts, so do not hang a quilt for more than three months, six at the most. Store it in a dark place for a while so the fibers can rest. If the quilt is wool, hang it for time periods shorter than three to six months to prevent drooping and stretching. Also, inspect the quilt for moths just as you would if the quilt were going to be stored.

Avoid hanging quilts where extreme temperatures and humidity are a problem. To reduce the chance of temperature variation, also avoid hanging them on an outside wall or near heating vents.

A room that is not constantly lighted is also beneficial because nothing is more harmful to textiles than light. Ultra-violet light damage is irreversible. It causes the breakdown of the dyes and pigments, accelerating the fading process. Direct sunlight is the worst, and fluorescent tube lighting is the second most damaging light source to dyes and fibers in textiles.

These light sources need to be filtered. Sunlight can be filtered by using mini-blinds, adjusting the slats down for the morning sun and up for the afternoon sun. Sheers on the windows are also a good filter. Beware of window films; the effective life of the film is five years. UV filters on fluorescent light tubes are recommended. The main objective is to cut out direct light rays on the fabrics. Remember, the industry standards for the colorfastness in today's quilting cottons in any light is only 20 hours maximum. This makes them very vulnerable.

When choosing a place to hang a quilt, remember that the quilt is safest the further away it is from a window. The worst wall is directly opposite a window. If possible, put the quilt on the same wall as the window. Morning light is the most harmful to the quilt. Look around the room and see where the light is hitting throughout the day. Avoid these areas.

If the quilt is on a bed in a sunny or bright room, I recommend you turn the quilt every morning. This prevents any one area from being over-exposed to a strong light source.

There are safe ways and poor ways to hang a quilt for display. Never hang a quilt using nails, staples, or pins. This creates severe stress in small areas and will break threads. It can also cause rust spots as well as sagging and distortion in the weave of the cloth. The weight of the quilt needs to be distributed over its entire width.

The most common way to hang today's quilts is to apply a hanging sleeve on the backside of the top width. Textile conservators offer the following tips for applying a sleeve:

1 Measure the top edge of the textile to be hung.

2 Cut a strip of twill tape or cotton webbing 4"-wide by the desired length minus $1/2$ inch. This should be wider than the finished width of the sleeve.

3 Make a casing (sleeve), cutting a strip of fabric 7"-wide by the desired length plus 1 inch. Fold and sew the long edge, right sides together. Turn right side out and turn the ends in and stitch. The casing should be narrower than the twill.

4 Stitch the casing to the twill, top and bottom, leaving a slight fullness or bubble extending outward. Do not stitch the ends.

5 Hand stitch the twill on all sides to the quilt back. Go through all layers of the quilt. The top row of stitches should be spaced $1/2$" apart, the bottom row spaced 1" apart to avoid tearing or puckering; be certain not to pull the stitches too tight.

Another excellent way to hang a quilt is by using a 2"-wide strip of Velcro® hook and loop tape. Measure the top edge of the quilt to be hung. Cut a prewashed 3"-wide strip of webbing or cotton fabric by the desired length but $^1/_2$" shorter than the actual top edge of the quilt. Machine stitch around all sides of the loop side of the tape to fasten it to the fabric support (Figure 15.13). Position the fabric support so that it is just below the top edge of the quilt, about $^1/_2$". It is important to keep the strip in a straight line, although the top edge of the quilt may not be straight.

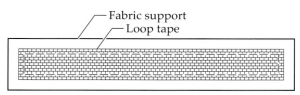

FIG. 15.13 *Stitch loop side to fabric support*

Hand sew the fabric support to the quilt at all sides. Stitch through all layers of the quilt. The top row of stitches should be spaced $^1/_2$" apart. The lower row may be spaced 1" apart. Use straight running stitches. Be careful not to pull the thread too tightly, as it may tear the fabric or cause puckering. Use only 100% cotton thread.

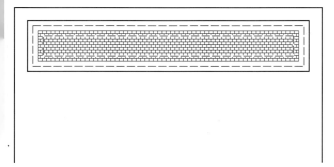

FIG. 15.14 *Stitch fabric support to quilt*

To mount the quilt on the wall, use a 1"x3" board that corresponds to the size of the top edge of the quilt. Seal it with polyurethane to prevent acid migration and discoloration of the quilt. Staple the hook side of the tape to the board (Figure 15.15). Attach the board to the wall. Press the top edge of the quilt to the loop side mounted on the board. Make adjustments if the quilt does not hang properly (Figure 15.16).

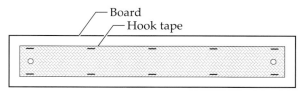

FIG. 15.15 *Staple hook side to mounting board*

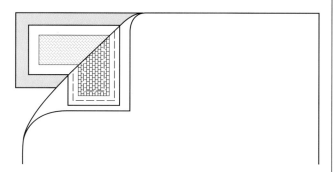

FIG. 15.16 *Attaching quilt to mounting board*

If the quilt is fragile or heavy, it will need extra support. This is especially true of old crazy quilts. Use a well-washed backing fabric and baste the quilt onto it. Run horizontal rows of hand basting stitches across the quilt and through the backing fabric about every 12" from the top to the bottom. Try to make the stitches invisible by following the pattern of the quilt top. Do not pull the stitches tight. Apply the sleeve to the quilt as discussed above. The backing fabric, not the quilt, should take the strain of hanging.

For maximum support, a backing fabric can be stretched over a wooden frame. The wood should be given a polyurethane finish to seal in the wood acids. Staple the backing fabric to the backside of the frame. Then baste the quilt to the backing fabric. The use of a curved needle is helpful.

There are several different types of rods for hanging quilts. If using any wood product such as a closet rod, dowel, or 1"x3" board, make sure that the wood has been sealed with polyurethane. You can also use a plexiglass rod or a decorative curtain rod.

We often have sections of quilts or pieced squares that we wish to frame and display under glass. To prepare the pieces, baste the piece to a cotton fabric on a wooden stretcher that fits inside the picture frame.

A spacer or mat is needed to prevent the glass from touching the fabric. This is very important because mold and mildew can grow where the fabric and glass touch. If glass is used on the front, allow for air circulation from the back. Instead of the paper usually applied to the back of the frame, staple a cotton dust cover over the back.

With proper care, your quilts can be on display and enjoyed for years. They deserve the same special consideration that any other piece of artwork would.

CONCLUSION

Today's quilters are finding it more and more difficult to find the time to produce the many quilts in their heads. We have developed and mastered machine piecing to compensate, but instead of gaining more quilts, we get more quilt tops done and then feel guilty for not finishing them.

Heirloom Machine Quilting is meant to be a means to an end. It is my sincere hope that this book will be the key to getting those tops finished and on the beds. If we continue to explore new and faster methods, we will keep quilting alive and well. Let the pictures inspire you to create your own heirloom-quality quilts in feasible amounts of time. Work through the exercises, and enjoy!

QUILTING
DESIGNS

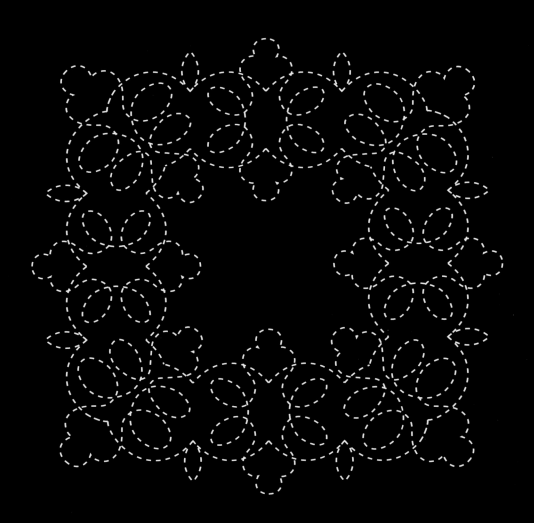

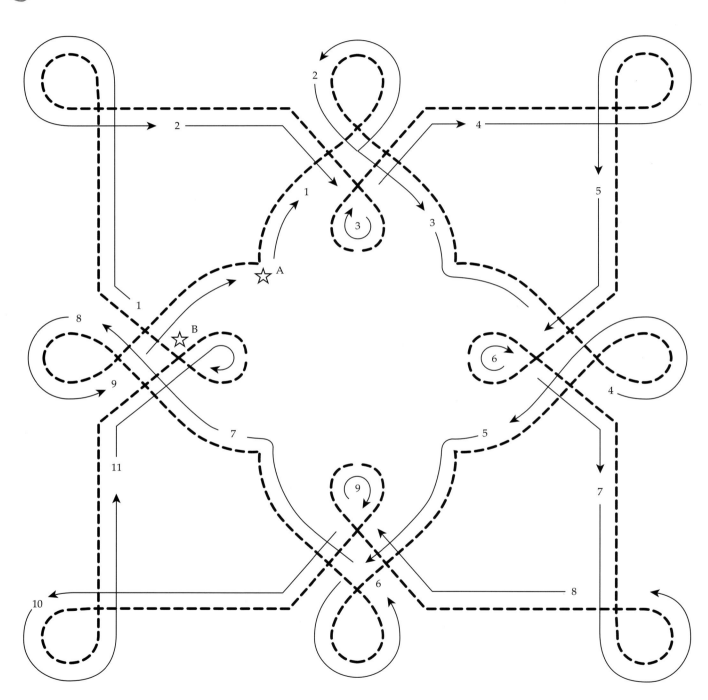

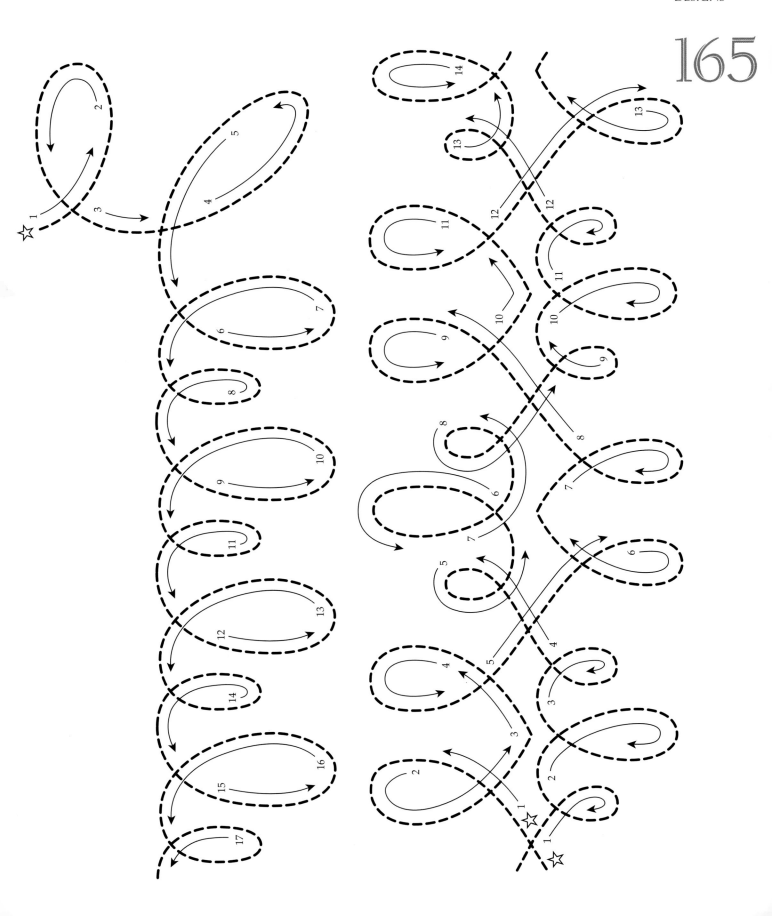

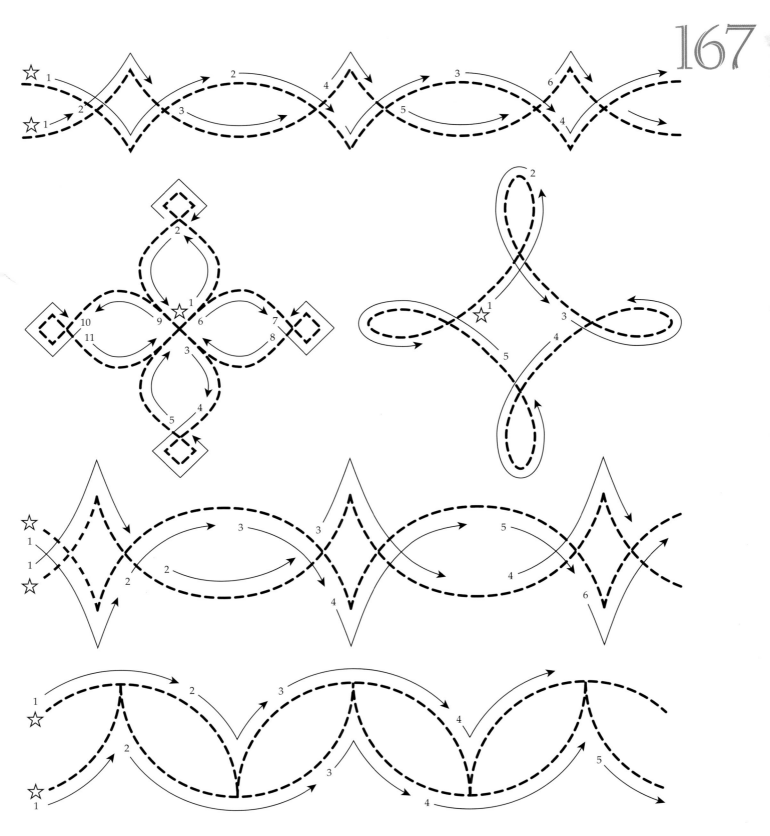

Quilt the first line to the end. Lock stitches.
Return to second line and quilt to the end.

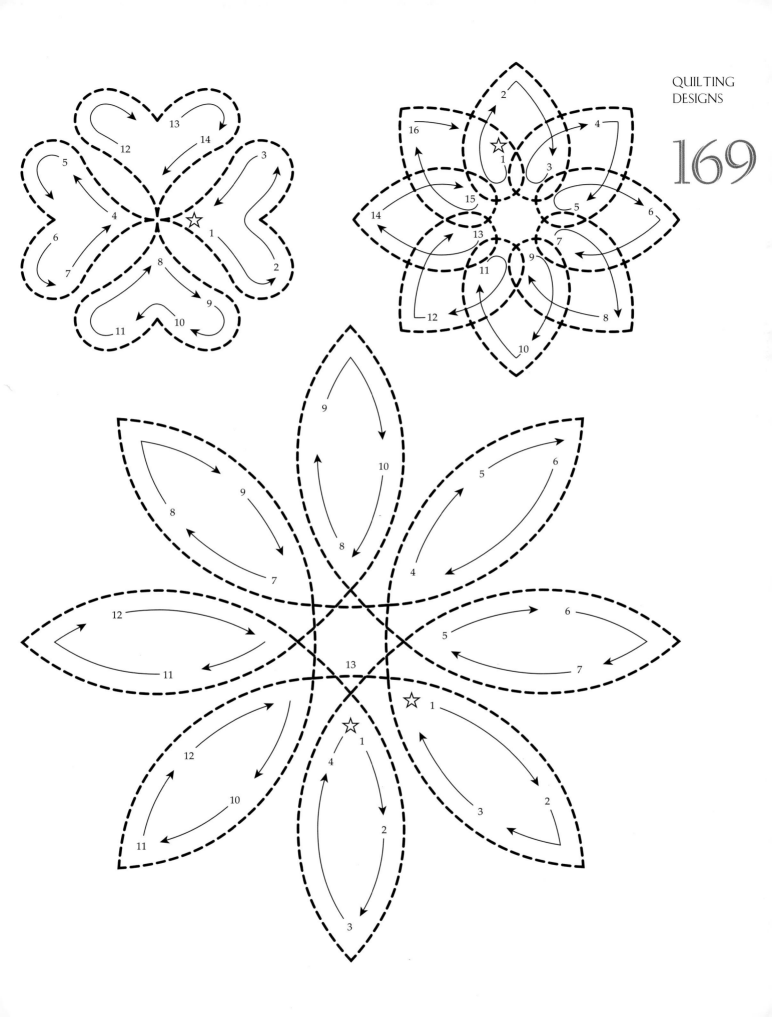

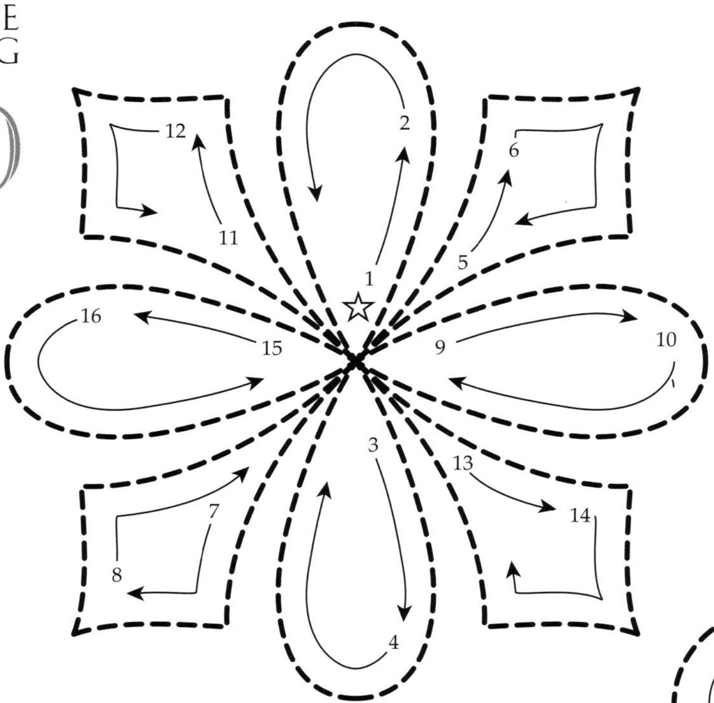
1
2
3
4
5
6
7
8
9
10
11
12
13
14
15
16

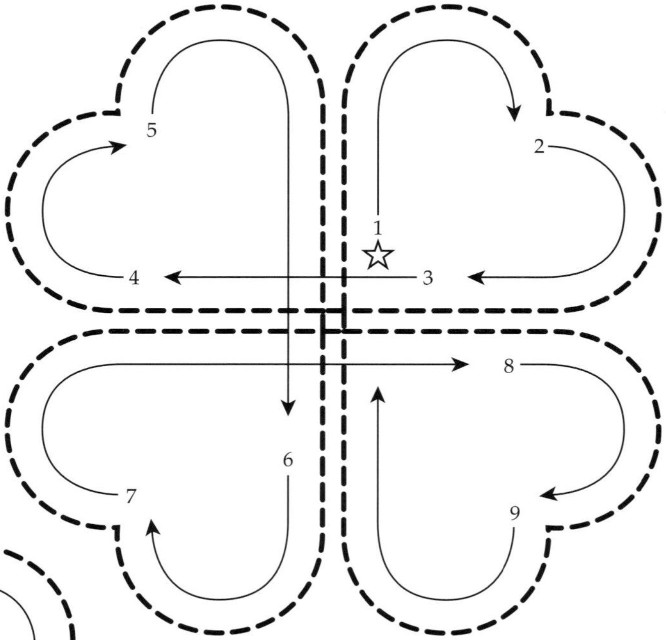
1
2
3
4
5
6
7
8
9

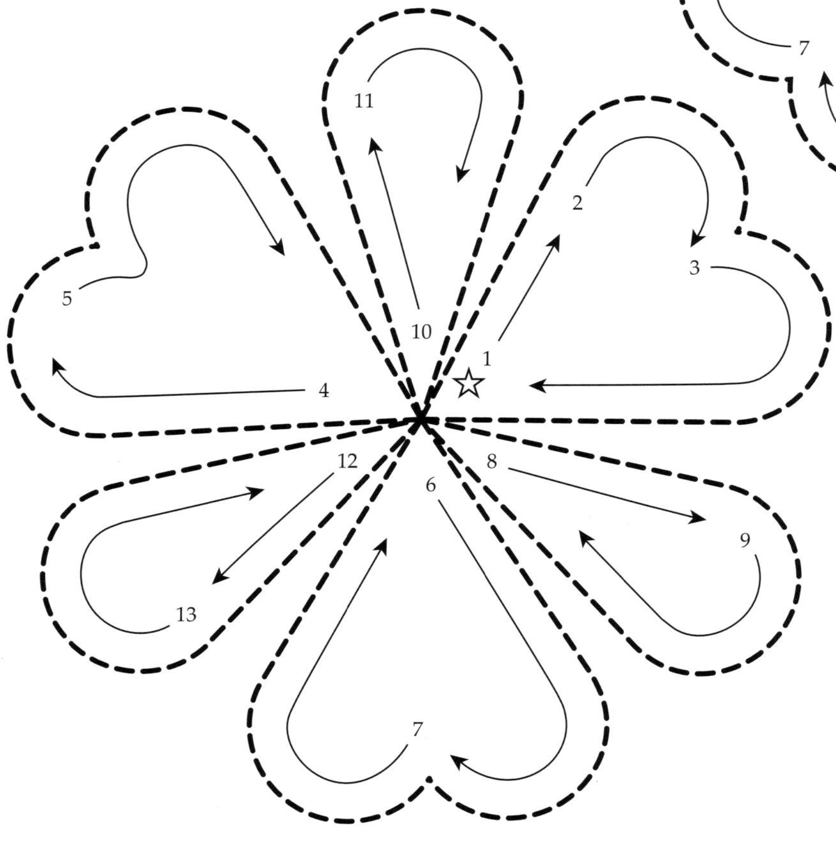
1
2
3
4
5
6
7
8
9
10
11
12
13

INDEX

173

ALSO FROM HARRIET HARGRAVE

Mastering Machine Appliqué
The Satin Stitch
by Harriet Hargrave

This book offers both beginning and advanced stitchers a complete guide to professional results in machine appliqué. It's really two books in one, with a flip/flop design so readers can easily distinguish between the two halves.

The first half is for users of the satin stitch, who often have different projects than the mock hand appliqué enthusiasts, who will flip to the second half of the book. While satin stitch is appropriate for washable garments, quilts, and accessories, the mock hand appliqué techniques find more use on delicate projects. Specific equipment, supplies, preparation methods, and techniques for each type of stitching are covered.

For more information on Harriet's book or any other C&T title write for a free catalog from:

C&T Publishing
P.O. Box 1456
Lafayette, CA 94553

WHOLESALE SUPPLIERS

*WHOLESALE SUPPLIERS for products
mentioned in this book:*

American Quilter   (stencil burner/hot pen)
P.O. Box 7455
Menlo Park, CA 94025

Bernina of America   (sewing cabinet and machine)
3500 Thayer Court
Aurora, IL 60504

C&T Publishing   (fine quilting books)
P.O. Box 1456
Lafayette, CA 94549

Fairfield Processing Corporation
P.O. Box 1130
Danbury, CT 06813

Inglis Publications Products   (DBK plastic)
P.O. Box 266
Dexter, MI 48130

Hobbs Bonded Fibers
P.O. Box 2521
Waco, TX 76702

Morning Glory Batting
The Reardon Company
P.O. Box 60056
Seattle, WA 98160-0056

Powell Publications   (quilting pattern books)
Box 513
Edmonds, WA 98020

Sew-Art International   (invisible thread, Tear-Away)
P.O. Box 550
Bountiful, UT 84010

The Stearns Technical Textile Co.   (batting and Ensure)
Mountain Mist Division
100 Williams Street
Cincinnati, OH   45215-6316

*Consumers can mail order all products mentioned in this
book directly from Harriet at:*

Harriet's Treadle Arts
6390 West 44th Ave.
Wheatridge, CO 80033
(303) 424-2742
(303) 424-1290 fax

BIBLIOGRAPHY

Beyer, Jinny
*The Art and Technique of
Creating Medallion Quilts*
McLean, Va.
EPM Publications, Inc., 1982

Cory, Pepper
Quilting Designs From The Amisch
Lafayette, Ca.
C & T Publishing, 1985

Donahue, Nancy
Quilting-As-You-Go Guide
Chino, Ca.
The Ink Spot, 1979

Emery, Linda Goodmon
A Treasury of Quilting Designs
Paducah, Ky.
The American Quilter's Society, 1990

Fanning, Robbie and Tony
The Complete Book Of Machine Quilting.
Radnor, Pa.
Chilton Book Co., 1980

Johannah, Barbara
*Continuous Curve Quilting
the Machine Pieced Quilt*
Menlo Park, Ca.
Pride of the Forest, 1980

Joseph, Marjory L.
Introductory Textile Science
New York
Holt, Rienhart and Winston, 1986

Macho, Linda
Quilting Patterns
New York
Dover Publications, 1984

Orlofsky, Patsy
The Quilt Digest 2
San Francisco
The Quilt Digest Press, 1984

Thompson, Shirley
The Finishing Touch
Edmonds, Wa.
Powell Publications, 1980

_____.
It's Not a Quilt Until It's Quilted
Edmonds, Wa.
Powell Publications, 1980

_____.
Old-Time Quilting Designs
Edmonds, Wa.
Powell Publications, 1989

Wyatt, Nancy Conlin.
"Textile Conservation Consultant"
Paris, Tx.
Photocopy

Zadel, Lauri Linch
"Wool Batts: From Sheep to Quilt"
Quilters Newsletter Magazine,
May 1986, page 34